Straight Talk About Teenage Pregnancy

Straight Talk About Teenage Pregnancy

Paula Edelson

Facts On File, Inc.

Straight Talk About Teenage Pregnancy

Copyright © 1999 by Paula Edelson

Facts On File, Inc.
11 Penn Plaza
New York NY 10001

Library of Congress Cataloging-in-Publication Data

Edelson, Paula.
    Straight talk about teenage pregnancy / Paula Edelson.
        p.   cm.
    Includes bibliographical references and index.
    Summary: Explains responsible sexual behavior, the ramifications of teenage pregnancy, ways to avoid it, and methods for coping with it, including various options.
        ISBN 0-8160-3717-5
        1. Teenage mothers—United States—Juvenile literature. 2. Teenage pregnancy—United States—Juvenile literature. [1. Pregnancy. 2. Teenage mothers.] I. Title.
    HQ759.4.E38   1998
    306.874'3—dc21   98-7268

Facts On File books are available at special discounts when purchased in bulk quantities for businesses, associations, institutions, or sales promotions. Please call our Special Sales Department in New York at (212) 967-8800 or (800) 322-8755.

You can find Facts On File on the World Wide Web at
http://www.factsonfile.com

Cover design and photograph by Smart Graphics

Printed in the United States of America

MP FOF 10 9 8 7 6 5 4 3 2

This book is printed on acid-free paper.

For Cliff,
Will,
and Nick

Contents

1

Young, Unwed, and Pregnant

Tess is 16. She lives at home with her mother and her two-year-old daughter, Stephanie. During the day Tess goes to school, and her mother stays with Stephanie. Then Tess comes home to be with her daughter, and her mother goes to work. On the weekends Tess works part-time to earn extra money. Tess used to like school and was a pretty good student. She used to think that she would go to college and maybe, if she worked hard enough, graduate school. English was her favorite subject, and she thought that maybe someday she would teach it.

All that changed when Stephanie came along. Now it's hard for Tess to find time for homework or reading, and she and her mother hardly ever see each other. It was even more difficult, though, the first few months of Stephanie's life. Then, Tess never slept; she was up all night with the

---

*Everyone identified by first name only in this book is a *composite*—a portrait drawn from details that come from many different people.

baby, at school during the day, and trying to do her homework whenever Stephanie took a nap. Needless to say, it was hard to stay awake in class and really hard to do a good job with her homework.

Trey's parents have always stayed out of his way. Maybe it's because he's got two older sisters who have always needed more attention, or maybe because by the time Trey came along, his parents were too tired and too old to spend a lot of energy worrying about him. Most of the time, Trey's happy with the way things are. He can come and go when he wants, and they never ask him where he's been. There are also times, however, when Trey could use someone at home to listen to him. Both his sisters have moved out and have families of their own, so Trey has gotten used to keeping things to himself.

He's never been crazy about school—classes have always bored him—but lately Trey's been looking forward to going there. There's a girl in his class that he can't stop looking at. Her name is Valerie. Trey's kind of known her for a while and never really thought much about her, but she's changed over the summer, and now Trey thinks she's hot. They always manage to end up sitting next to each other in the classes they're in together. Trey asked her out a couple of days ago: They're going to the movies on Friday night. It's the first date Trey's had in a while, and he's definitely psyched.

Tonya and Jack: Together forever, best friends, totally in love—everyone knows it. What everyone *doesn't* know is that they haven't slept together, which is pretty surprising, considering that Tonya and Jack have been going out for three years.

When the two of them first started going out, back when they were 15, Jack used to pressure Tonya to have sex. But Tonya wasn't ready, and she told him so. They went through some hard times over this. They had lots of arguments, and they almost broke up. But in the end Jack realized that he'd rather be with Tonya than with anyone else, and that's where they've left it.

Robin hates high school. Classes are boring, and if you were to ask her, she'd tell you that she doesn't see why she needs to learn any of this stuff. What she really likes to do is to go out to clubs with her friends. In fact, it was at a club that she met Matt. He's 25, which Robin thinks is really cool. Because he's 10 years older than Robin, he's more experienced in all sorts of ways. "He knows what he's doing," she tells her friends. "I can really trust him."

Soon Robin and Matt are sleeping together. At first it hurt Robin to have sex, but now it's not so bad. Sometimes they remember to use a condom, and sometimes they don't. Robin doesn't worry much about it. If I get pregnant, she thinks, I'll deal with it. Matt's older—he'll know what to do.

Every year, 1 million teenagers in the United States get pregnant. About half of them give birth. That means that annually, 500,000 babies are born to mothers who are under 20, usually unmarried, and often still in high school. This may not surprise you; you may have friends your own age who have had babies, or perhaps you have one yourself.

Many of these babies grow up feeling loved and cared for, with parents who thoroughly enjoy the experience of raising a child. On the other hand, many teen parents find that having a baby at this time of life is really difficult. For one thing, as Tess knows, babies are really expensive.

In addition, raising a child takes up a lot of time. Unlike a job or school, you can't just turn your back on a child at the end of the day. You—or someone—has to be there 24 hours a day. Someone has to be awake whenever the baby is, holding the baby until you figure out why he or she is crying, comforting the baby until the crying stops. That can be difficult even for adults who are married and settled in their lives. For teenagers, who are still growing both physically and emotionally, this task can be overwhelming.

Finally, because parenting is so expensive and time-consuming, it's difficult for teen parents to find the time or the money to pursue their own careers. A lot of teenagers don't think much about this when they get pregnant, but it can be a big issue later on. Tess, for example, does not think she'll be able to afford college after she graduates from high school. And even if she could afford it, she's worried that she won't have the time, energy, or concentration to keep up with the work. Many teenagers who have had children —33 percent of all been parents, according to the Alan Guttmacher Institute—end up dropping out of high school completely before they have earned their diplomas.

How Does Pregnancy Happen?

In order to understand the issues surrounding pregnancy, it's important to know how pregnancy occurs to begin with. You may be surprised at how much you don't know about reproduction. Here's a basic overview of how it works.

The Male Reproductive System

Reproduction happens when the sperm from a man's penis penetrates the outer covering of a woman's egg, or ovum. (You'll find out in the following pages about women's eggs.) The sperm are made by the male reproductive system and are ejaculated into the woman's body when a man and woman have sexual intercourse.

Take a look at the figure on page 5. The parts of the male reproductive system that can be seen from the outside are the penis and the scrotum, which is a loose sac underneath the penis. Inside the scrotum are two organs called testes, which produce the sperm.

Male Reproductive System

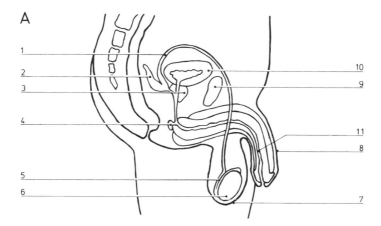

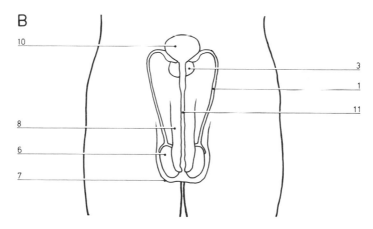

A	Median section through the male pelvis	3	Prostate gland
		4	Cowper's glands
		5	Epididymis
B	Anterior view of the male reproductive tract	6	Testis
		7	Scrotum
		8	Penis
		9	Pubic symphysis
1	Vas deferens	10	Bladder
2	Seminal vesicle	11	Urethra

© DIAGRAM

Actually, the testes have two functions. The first is to make sperm. This is done extremely quickly: Believe it or not, testes produce about 50,000 sperm every minute. The other function of the testes is to manufacture a hormone called testosterone. This hormone makes the production of sperm by the testes possible. Testosterone is also responsible for the changes in a boy's body as he reaches puberty. These changes include the growth of pubic, body, and facial hair; denser bones; bigger muscles; and a deeper voice.

Once the sperm are made, they travel from the scrotum to a structure at the top of the testes called the epididymis. While in the epididymis the sperm mature, a process that takes about 2 to 10 days. After this process, the sperm travel from the testes to the penis through two tubes called the vasa deferentia. During this journey the sperm pass through glands that produce fluids to nurture and protect the sperm. This fluid together with the sperm is called the semen.

The semen enters the woman's body through the penis. When a man becomes sexually excited, the penis becomes bigger, longer, and firmer. This is known as an erection, and it is what makes it possible for the penis to enter the woman's vagina. During sexual intercourse, when a man reaches orgasm, or the height of sexual excitement, his penis ejaculates, which means that the muscles around the penis contract, sending semen containing sperm out of the penis and into the woman's vagina.

Once inside the body, the semen travel toward the woman's egg. Semen contains between 30 million and 300 million sperm, so it's somewhat surprising that only one, if any, sperm actually comes in contact with the egg. But this is indeed what happens; the rest of the sperm either die on the way—getting caught in the mucous membranes of the vagina—or serve as helpers for the one sperm that will fertilize the egg by loosening the layer of cells surrounding the egg. As soon as one sperm penetrates the egg's outer covering and fertilizes the egg, the remainder of the sperm build a protective layer that keeps other sperm from getting through and joining the egg.

The Female Reproductive System

The main functions of the female reproductive system are to manufacture an egg that can be fertilized and then to provide a place for that fertilized egg to grow and develop into a baby. This developmental phase takes about nine months from the time the egg is fertilized until the day a new baby is born.

The figure on page 8 gives you an idea of how complex the female reproductive system is. Unlike the parts of the male reproductive system, most of the female reproductive system's parts cannot be seen from the outside. Those that are visible from the outside are as a unit referred to as the vulva. The vulva includes the pubic bone; the mons pubis, which is the fatty tissue that acts as padding in front of the pubic bone; and the labia majora, outer folds of skin.

Inside the labia majora are two folds of skin called the labia minora. Connected to these folds is the clitoris, the part of a woman's body that is the source of sexual excitement. Like the penis, the clitoris becomes erect when a woman is sexually excited.

The rest of the female reproductive system is located inside the woman's body. First there is the vagina, which is a passageway connecting the outside of the body to the crucial organs inside. At the end of the vagina is the cervix. When the penis ejaculates semen into the woman's vagina, the sperm travel through a small opening in the cervix to the uterus.

The ovaries, which are located on each side of the abdomen, are similar to a man's testes in that they produce sex hormones. Called progesterone and estrogen, these hormones stimulate the development of breasts, pubic and body hair, and rounder hips and body shape when a girl reaches puberty. The ovaries also produce eggs, but unlike sperm, which are produced and travel by the thousands,

External Female Genitals

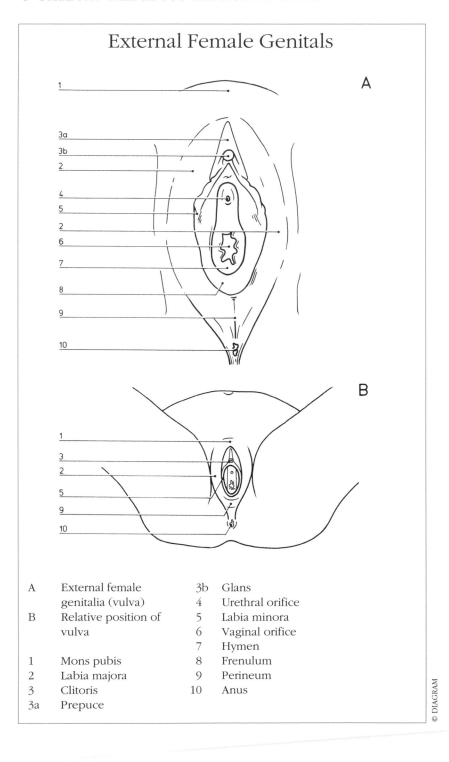

A	External female genitalia (vulva)	3b	Glans
B	Relative position of vulva	4	Urethral orifice
		5	Labia minora
		6	Vaginal orifice
		7	Hymen
1	Mons pubis	8	Frenulum
2	Labia majora	9	Perineum
3	Clitoris	10	Anus
3a	Prepuce		

only one egg is released by the ovaries each month. The process of releasing an egg from an ovary is called ovulation. Upon completion of ovulation, the egg is ready to be fertilized by a sperm.

After the ovaries release the mature egg, it travels from the ovary through one of the connecting fallopian tubes into the uterus. This journey takes about four or five days. During the last part of this process—while the egg is still in the fallopian tube—it goes through a 12-to-24-hour phase during which it can be fertilized by a sperm. If the egg is not fertilized during this time, it begins to break down and becomes infertile. Whether or not it is fertilized by a sperm, the egg does reach the uterus. If it has been fertilized, it will remain in the uterus to develop into a baby. If it is unfertilized, it dissolves.

In the meantime, the uterus goes through a process each month that prepares it for the entrance of a fertilized egg. This process is called the menstrual cycle. During this time the uterus lining thickens, again in preparation for a fertilized egg. If a fertilized egg does enter the uterus, the thickened lining remains. If the egg that enters the uterus is not fertilized, the lining breaks down and is released through the woman's vagina. The release of the lining—called the menstrual period—takes about five days. It signals the end of the monthly menstrual cycle.

Embryo to Baby

About a day and a half after an egg has been fertilized, it divides into two cells and becomes an embryo, which then embeds itself in the uterus lining. Ten days or so after this happens, it becomes buried within the uterine wall, in a process called implantation.

Once this occurs, the embryo begins to draw from the mother the food and oxygen it needs to survive and grow. It is able to do this through a structure called the placenta, which is embedded in the uterus wall. The placenta is connected to the embryo through the umbilical cord.

With the help of the nutrients and oxygen it receives from the mother via the placenta and umbilical cord, the embryo develops fairly rapidly. The first organs to form are the heart and brain, followed by the eyes and face. Arms and legs, as well as the liver, lungs, and stomach soon form. Once the embryo is nine weeks old, all of its major organs are developing. The embryo is now known as a fetus. By the end of 12 weeks, the fetus is about 4 inches long, and bones are forming. By 18 weeks, the mother can usually feel the fetus moving. At 24 weeks the baby is considered viable, which means that with medical assistance it can survive outside the mother's uterus. At 30 weeks the eyes can see.

At 40 weeks, the baby is fully developed and is ready to be born. Some babies are born slightly before 40 weeks—most medical professionals consider a baby to be full term by 38 weeks. Some babies are not born until they are as old as 42 weeks. Labor can take anywhere from 2 hours to 36 hours. It begins with slight contractions that become stronger and closer together. These contractions serve to thin and dilate the cervix as the baby makes its way down from the uterus and then through the vagina. At long last, the baby is born.

Why Do Teenagers Get Pregnant?

If having children is so difficult, time-consuming, and expensive—getting back to a point raised earlier—why do so many teenagers find themselves becoming parents? There's no easy answer to this question, but there are two very important factors that can give us a good place to start. First, more teenagers than ever before are now becoming sexually active at an early age. According to a 1995 study by the U.S. Department of Health and Human Services, slightly more than half of U.S. girls and nearly two-thirds of U.S. boys have had sex by their 18th birthday.

Second, few teenagers use contraceptives, or birth control, and many use the birth-control method they have chosen incorrectly. The same 1995 study from the U.S. Department of Health and Human Services reveals that 35 percent of all sexually active teenagers—more than one-third of this group—do not use any contraceptives at all during their first sexual experience. Many teenagers don't use birth control for up to a year after their first sexual experience. Since it's easier for teenagers to get pregnant than any other age group, that's a whole year of taking very big chances. Considering that 70 percent of all teenage pregnancies occur during unprotected sexual intercourse, it's easy to see that not using birth control can easily lead to pregnancy. It is interesting to note that while adolescents in the United States have a lower rate of sexual intercourse than teenagers in many European nations, actually, the United States has the highest teen pregnancy rate of any developed country. It is twice as high as the rates in England, France, and Canada, three times as high as in Sweden, and four times as high as in the Netherlands, according to 1998 statistics compiled by the Alan Guttmacher Institute.

These statistics and patterns of behavior do not mean that most teen girls who become pregnant do it on purpose. Actually, the vast majority of teen pregnancies happen by accident—only 14 percent of teen parents planned to become pregnant, according to Child Trends, a Washington, D.C., health organization. But the human body is designed to create children. If young, healthy teenagers are having sex without correctly using birth control to prevent pregnancy, they are very likely to end up with a pregnancy to deal with.

Of course, some teenagers choose not to become sexually active, either to be sure of not getting pregnant or for some other reason. Tonya, for example, has decided that she wants to wait before having sex with Jack. She enjoys her physical relationship with him, but they've concentrated on sexual activity that won't lead to pregnancy—kissing and petting.

And some teenagers who do become sexually active are very careful about using contraceptives according to the directions. Even in this case, it's still possible to get pregnant —sometimes contraceptives just don't work or the people using them make mistakes—but using birth control certainly lowers the risk of pregnancy, even if it does not completely eliminate it.

Making Decisions About Sex

It's hard to know why some teenagers choose to have sexual intercourse earlier than others. Some people feel they're in love and are ready to show that love sexually. Others are curious or adventurous. Some people don't think much about it until it actually happens. Robin, who started sleeping with Matt soon after they began seeing each other, didn't really seriously consider what having sex would mean emotionally or of its physical consequences. She just really wanted to be with Matt. She was very attracted to him and found herself thinking about kissing and touching him all the time. She also knew in her head that if *she* didn't sleep with him, he'd just find someone else who would.

Despite the many reasons, there are certain characteristics that do seem to increase a young person's chances of engaging in sexual intercourse, which in turn makes them susceptible to pregnancy. For example, studies show that teenagers who use alcohol, tobacco, or other drugs are more likely to become sexually active than those who don't. Studies also show that the neighborhoods teenagers grow up in play a role in the decisions they make about becoming sexually active. According to *Dubious Conceptions,* Kristin Luker's 1996 book about teenage pregnancy, teenagers who grow up in poorer neighborhoods, for example, have a 36 percent higher chance of engaging in sexual activity than do those who come from more affluent areas.

Then there are factors that are a little harder to measure, but that are extremely important. Peer pressure is one of the most significant of these factors. The simple truth is that because so many teens are already sexually active, a lot of young people feel a sense of urgency—either from themselves or from their friends—to become sexually active as well. Valerie, for example, is the only virgin she knows of in her class. Everyone else she knows has already had sex —or talks like they have. Valerie feels left out of a lot of their conversations. And sometimes her classmates make her feel like a complete drag. "Come on, get with it," they tell her. At times like these, Valerie feels that if something doesn't happen soon, she may have to lie to her friends, and say that it did.

Pressure can also come from a teenager's boyfriend or girlfriend. Relationships are sometimes threatened when one person demands sexual intercourse from the other. There are ways to handle this type of pressure, but it's not always an easy thing to do. For more on this, see Chapter 2.

Then there are the psychosocial and physiological reasons for teenagers wanting to have sex. The hormones that develop during adolescence do cause an awakening of sexual awareness and desire, in both males and females. It's completely normal for teenagers to want to explore and act on sexual feelings.

In addition, many teenagers don't give much thought to what might happen if they do decide to become sexually active. The fact that sex can lead to unplanned pregnancy is not always first in their minds. When Robin first had sex, the main thing she was thinking was how glad she was that she had finally done it. Once again, the risks she was taking —getting pregnant, contracting a sexually transmitted disease—just didn't seem as important as being with Matt. In addition, eventually Robin enjoyed sex with Matt—it's always made her feel really good.

Likewise, many teenagers feel a sense of invulnerability. They may know about the risks associated with the behaviors they choose—drinking alcohol, smoking cigarettes, doing drugs, or having sexual intercourse—but feel that they'll be careful or lucky enough to avoid getting into any trouble.

Media Messages

Teens' attitudes toward teen pregnancy don't just arise from their own feelings. A lot of factors affect how teens think and feel about teen pregnancy. For example, magazine ads, movies, commercials, and television programs all have a tremendous influence on the way all of us—teens and adults—choose to behave.

Take tobacco use. On the one hand, scientists and doctors tell us that smoking or chewing tobacco is a dangerous habit that can cause illness and death. On the other, billboard and magazine advertisements show us people who are always healthy, beautiful, and active. One would think from these advertisements that smoking or chewing tobacco is actually a glamorous, even healthy, thing to do.

The same can be said for the way people who are pregnant or who have babies are sometimes portrayed in movies or television programs. Take a movie like *Baby Boom,* which is about a business executive who becomes a parent overnight to a three-month-old baby left to her care by a distant relative. The executive ultimately chooses the baby over her career, moves blissfully to Vermont, and stumbles on an award-winning recipe for baby food. Another movie about people who become parents overnight is *Three Men and a Baby,* which is about three handsome bachelors who discover a baby on their doorstep. After a series of funny trials and tribulations, all four members of this unusual household settle down to an amusing and even enviable lifestyle. Who wouldn't think, from seeing these movies, that being a parent is easy?

Unfortunately, that usually isn't the case, particularly when the parents are teenagers. In real life, teenage parents will almost never use the words *easy* or *glamorous* to describe their lives. In truth, being a parent is neither.

A Reason to Hope

More than a few young people in America have a sense of hopelessness about their future. They may have grown up surrounded by violence. Maybe they come from abusive homes, or perhaps they come from neighborhoods where young people belong to gangs, and where crime and killings happen on a regular basis. Why, they may ask themselves, should I worry about my future when I may not be around to enjoy it? Or if they're neglected or abused by their families, they may look to a child to give them the love they've been deprived of growing up.

These are all completely understandable feelings. There are no easy answers to issues of crime, poverty, and domestic violence, and the effects that they have on people who grow up surrounded by them. If you're in this kind of a situation, know that you have an absolute right to feel the way you do. And of course there's really nothing you can do to change what has happened in the past. Anyone in your situation would feel the pain and hopelessness you feel. Maybe, though, there are ways to change your future. It could be that you have more options than you are aware of. Perhaps with some help and support, there are opportunities you can find that might give you the future you want. It may be easier for you to find those opportunities if you decide that it's worth the effort to protect yourself from becoming pregnant. In the long run, it may be the best thing you can do not only for yourself but for the children you may someday have.

The Consequences of Sexual Intercourse

Like many things in life, sexual intercourse can be a lot of fun—and it can also have consequences that are not so much fun. Think for a moment about Tess and her situation. Tess loves Stephanie dearly, but she also wonders at times if maybe it would have been better if she had waited to have children. But Tess was in love with her boyfriend, Rob, and was so wrapped up in him that she put her own hesitations and fears about what they were doing aside. So when they had sexual intercourse and it was too much trouble to use contraceptives—it was too hard to remember to get them, or they didn't want to break the mood, or it made Tess uncomfortable to keep insisting on something Rob didn't like very much—they went ahead and had unprotected sex.

In fact, most cases of teen pregnancy occur as Tess's did —as a result of unprotected sexual intercourse. According to the Alan Guttmacher Institute, a sexually active teenage girl who does *not* use contraceptives has a 90 percent chance of getting pregnant within a year. Even when contraceptives *are* used correctly, pregnancy can still occur. (You can find out more about contraceptives and how to prevent pregnancy in general in Chapter 3.)

Getting pregnant isn't the only problem associated with sexual intercourse. Every year, according to a 1995 Planned Parenthood study, more than 100,000 teenagers contract a sexually transmitted disease, such as syphilis, gonorrhea, herpes, or chlamydia. And HIV (human immunodeficiency virus), the virus that causes AIDS, which was in 1996 the seventh leading killer of young people ages 15–24, according to the National Center for Health Statistics, is most commonly transmitted in that age group through sexual intercourse.

Last but certainly not least, there are emotional consequences of having sexual intercourse. This intimate act can
leave a person feeling extremely vulnerable, particularly
early in a relationship. Some people have found that
engaging in sexual intercourse too soon can even destroy
a relationship—particularly if one of the people involved
was not ready to become sexually active in the first place.

The consequences of engaging in sexual intercourse—
and of its alternative behavior, practicing abstinence—will
be discussed more fully in Chapters 2 and 3. For the time
being, it's enough to know that having sex—with or without
using contraceptives—can cause pregnancy and that the
only sure protection against becoming pregnant is to
abstain from this behavior.

Young Women and Older Men
Often the phrase "teen pregnancy" is misleading, since
many of the fathers are far from teenagers. Robin feels
flattered that a 25-year-old guy would be interested in her,
but her situation is actually very common among teenage
girls who do become pregnant.

In fact, the majority of babies born to teenage girls were
fathered by older men. According to a 1996 study done by
Child Trends, two-thirds of all U.S. babies born to mothers
under the age of 19 are fathered by men over the age of
20. This is important to know because a young woman
involved with an older man may think that if the guy is
older, he somehow knows more about sex and is more
responsible than someone younger. Unfortunately, that's
not necessarily true.

Sometimes younger women get pregnant because
they've been raped by older men. According to a study of
selected high school students, reported in *Dubious Conceptions*, Kristin Luker's 1996 book about teenage pregnancy,
about 7 percent of all teenage girls surveyed have admitted
that at one time or another they were forced to have sex
against their will. Among those girls who had had sex

before they were 15 years old, the figure was 60 percent. Even more startling is a statistic compiled by the National Center on Child Abuse and Neglect in 1992. This organization's study surveyed a large and diverse group of mothers who had become pregnant as teenagers. About half these women, the study found, had been the victims of rape.

A thorough discussion of date or acquaintance rape is beyond the scope of this book, but if you or someone you know has been forced to have sex, there are places you can go to get help. The resources listed on page 127–128 of this book offer a good place to start. (You might also take a look at *Straight Talk About Date Rape,* by Susan Mufson, C.S.W., and Rachel Kranz.)

Teen Pregnancy and Society

Teenagers who get pregnant are young people who suddenly have to make very grown-up decisions. The choices they face are very complex. No matter what they decide to do, they—and often their families—will always be affected, in one way or the other, by the experience.

Teen pregnancy also takes a toll on society in general. This cost is measured in several ways. To begin with, many teen pregnancies are paid for in one way or another by tax dollars. And according to a fact sheet on teen pregnancy compiled by the Alan Guttmacher Institute in 1998, teen pregnancy costs U.S. taxpayers between $25 and $50 billion each year.

Those dollars pay for many of the necessary programs and procedures associated with teen pregnancy. For example, many teenagers can't afford to pay for their own prenatal care, the medical attention they get while they're pregnant. The care that they receive at clinics or doctors' offices is often funded through tax dollars.

In addition, many teen parents can't afford to pay for daycare for their babies if they choose to go back to school.

Some, like Tess, leave their children in the care of family members. But others don't have that option. Fortunately for them, several federally and state-funded child-care options do exist. These centers provide important options for teenagers and good care for their children, but they are expensive, and again, they are paid for through tax dollars.

Some people believe that society should help bear the cost of teen pregnancies in this country. They believe that society is better off when all parents and children get the help, education, and health care that they need. There are others, however, who resent having to pay for what they may feel are other people's problems and other people's mistakes.

How do you feel about this issue? Keep in mind that every adult with a legal job in the United States has to pay taxes. This means that not only people who have plenty of money but poor people who struggle to make ends meet must contribute money to pay for teen pregnancy. On the other hand, according to the Alan Guttmacher Institute, the social costs of teen pregnancy totals between $25 and $50 billion, or about 1 to 2 percent of the federal budget. This amounts to between 10¢ and 20¢ per citizen. Do you think this figure should be higher, lower, or zero?

The Welfare Debate

In the past, many teen parents have relied on welfare payments to help them raise their children. Welfare is a government-based program that gives money to people who need it. Teen parents, who are usually less well-off that those who have children after they've completed their high school and college studies, have for many years been prime candidates for welfare aid. According to *Dubious Conceptions,* families born from teenage parents represent half of all families who are or have been on welfare.

Some people believe that welfare has not been a helpful aid to teenage parents, because, in their view, it promotes the wrong message. One such group, a conservative think-tank called The Heritage Foundation, published a study called *Combating Illegitimacy and Counseling Teen Absti-nence: A Key Component of Welfare Reform* in 1995. The study voices concern that giving state money to single mothers (which many teenage mothers are) is a signal to all teenagers that an unmarried teenager is every bit as capable of raising a healthy, happy child as parents who are married. Such a message, the study says, could well encourage other teenagers to become pregnant as well.

Others argue that such a fear is not well founded. *Dubious Conceptions,* for example, stresses that teenagers are not as dependent on welfare as some people fear. According to this book, teenagers account for fewer than 10 percent of people on welfare at any given time. In addition, almost three-quarters of the teenagers who collected welfare payments did so for a period of three years or less. Moreover, Luker argues, the vast majority of teenagers who get pregnant do not do so because they intend to collect a welfare check (which is often not high enough to support a mother and child). Instead, teen preg-nancy is something that most often happens by accident and without intention.

In 1996 President Bill Clinton signed into law a piece of legislation calling for major changes in the welfare system. The law placed certain conditions on teenage parents who want to collect welfare. These teenagers must now (1) stay in school and prepare for future employment and (2) live with their parents until the age of 21. Teenagers who come from abusive homes can qualify for welfare if they live in a specially supervised residence. For more on this, see the discussion of second chance homes on pages 114–115.

In addition, the new law states that regardless of their situation, teenagers can receive welfare for a total of five years (or less, depending on state policy). Think for a moment about the welfare situation. Do you think it's a fair plan? Do you think it sends the wrong message to teenag-ers? Do you think the new law will help prevent teenagers from becoming pregnant?

Teen Parents

Tess never thought much about how expensive having a child could be—until Stephanic came home from the hospital. Suddenly there was a new mouth to feed and loads of diapers to buy. Even now, Stephanie never seems to stop growing. Practically every month she needs new clothes. She outgrows her shoes in just a few weeks, and each season she's ready for another jacket or coat.

Money is only one of the issues teen parents face. In addition, there is the concern of education and opportunity. Like some teenage parents, Tess—with the help of her parents—has figured out a way to finish high school. But she also knows that she'll have to put aside her dream of getting scholarships to go to college and law school, for at least the time being.

Finally, teens who become parents find that having a child is a full-time commitment. Aside from the endless hours—night and day—that she spends caring for Stephanie, Tess can't remember the last time she saw a movie that wasn't a children's cartoon. She never gets to go to her friends' parties, or even to go out for pizza with them after school. When Tess thinks about the difference between her life now and the way it was before Stephanie was born, she can't believe it. Now she sees that being a teen parent involves tremendous sacrifices—and the demands do not end until the child is old enough to be legally independent. (For more information about the situations teen parents face, see Chapter 5.)

The Children of Teenagers

Teenagers who have children don't always make terrific parents, for several reasons. To begin with, there are many difficulties associated with being a teen parent. Being a parent of any age takes a great deal of maturity, selflessness, and sacrifice. It is difficult to put a child's needs first at any age, but it may be even harder for teenagers, who still have strong needs of their own that are hard to put aside.

Studies also show that the babies of teenagers are less likely to receive adequate prenatal or pediatric care and, for that reason, are less healthy than the children of older parents. One reason for this statistic may be that, as you have learned, most teenagers who become pregnant do so by accident: According to the 1996 *Child Trends* study only 14 percent of teenagers who become pregnant did so intentionally. According to statistics compiled in 1998 by the Alan Guttmacher Institute, pregnant teens are the least likely of all maternal ages to get early and regular care. For this reason, the same Guttmacher fact sheet reports, a teenage mother is more at risk of pregnancy complications such as premature or prolonged labor, anemia, and high blood pressure. The risks are even greater for teens who are less than 15 years old.

Preventing Pregnancy

In some ways, preventing pregnancy takes almost as much responsibility as raising a child does, although it's not nearly as difficult. Most teenagers who have children did not want to become parents—they just did not follow the basic rule needed to keep a pregnancy from occurring.

That basic rule is to practice abstinence, which means to avoid having sexual intercourse. Couples who don't abstain from sex can lessen their chances of getting pregnant by using birth control correctly and responsibly—that means *every single time* they have sex. But even though contraceptives can be effective when used properly, pregnancy can still occur. Abstinence is not always an easy choice for a couple to make, but it can be done. The next chapter offers some advice on ways to practice this only sure means of birth control.

2

Delaying Sexual Intercourse

Tess often thinks about how it was when she first started seeing Rob, Stephanie's father. She remembers how excited she was whenever he called, how she'd drop everything to go out with him. Before too long, Rob made it pretty clear to Tess that he wanted to have sex with her. And Tess soon found herself avoiding his caresses and kisses—not because she didn't want him to touch her, but because she worried that she wouldn't be able to stop him from going too far.

Finally one day, Rob asked her what was going on. "Don't you like me anymore?" he said. Tess answered yes, of course she did. "Then what's the problem?" he wanted to know.

Tess mumbled something about not feeling well. But she knew that sooner or later she would either have to tell Rob that she was a virgin and that she wasn't ready to have sex or she'd just have to keep her nervousness to herself and sleep with him. Tess always imagined having the guts to tell Rob to slow down, asking him to give her time, telling him that she would rather not deal with this whole thing for a while. But deep down she was scared of losing him, so she never said anything, even after they'd begun having sex.

Now, when Tess thinks about how she behaved just two years ago, she can't believe it. Was that really me?, she wonders. Why couldn't I just tell him I wasn't ready?

Tonya has always been pretty straightforward with Jack about sex. "No, I haven't done it yet," she told him on their first date. "And no, it's not something I think I'll be doing for quite a while. Not until I'm married, or at least in love with someone."

Jack listened to her but wasn't sure he believed her. But he didn't begin to pressure her to have sex with him until after they'd been dating for about three months. Then he told her he wanted to, and that he wasn't sure how much longer he could wait for her. "Everyone's doing it, Tonya," he said. "Everyone except you and me. Come on—it's not that big of a deal."

Tonya was upset—she thought Jack knew where she stood on this. Now he was making her feel like a prude. And of course, she didn't want to lose Jack, either. But he wasn't the only one with strong feelings about sex. The problem was that they completely disagreed. They'd have to reach an understanding, Tonya knew, or the relationship would be over.

There are several ways to lessen a person's chances of becoming pregnant, but there is only one method that completely eliminates the risk. That strategy is called *abstinence,* or avoiding all forms of sexual intimacy. Of course, it's easy to tell teenagers to "just say no." The hard part is knowing how to abstain when a boyfriend or girlfriend is pressuring you and when all of your friends are doing it.

The first thing you need to know about practicing sexual abstinence is that it's a decision you do have control over. If you don't want to have sex with someone because you're not attracted to him or her in that way, because you don't want to risk becoming pregnant, or because you're simply not ready to take that step, you can make that choice successfully. This chapter will give you the tools and knowledge you need to do so, but it is ultimately up to you to carry it through—no one else can do it for you.

Reasons to Practice Sexual Abstinence

If you're not sure how you feel about practicing abstinence, there are a couple of issues surrounding it that you may want to consider.

Even though it's true that people are sexually active at a younger age than ever before, there are also many young people who choose to remain abstinent until they are involved in a mature and monogamous relationship such as marriage. Some of these teenagers have made this choice because they know it's the only absolutely sure form of protection against pregnancy. They're concerned that raising a child before they're ready to become a parent is unfair not only to themselves but to the child as well. And, of course, sexual abstinence is also the only absolutely sure protection against sexually transmitted diseases.

But there are other reasons teenagers choose abstinence as well. Some young people choose to abstain from sex because of their religious beliefs. Many religions frown on sexual intercourse outside marriage. Other teens believe that rather than bringing a couple closer together, sexual intercourse can actually ruin a romantic relationship if it's engaged in too soon. Finally, there are those who choose not to become sexually active because they feel it is morally wrong to do so outside of marriage.

There are no right or wrong answers to the abstinence question. Again, it is a decision you have to make for yourself. And, as with all decisions, there are consequences to whatever choice you end up making. Learning to weigh the advantages and disadvantages of a choice you have to make is called making a responsible decision. You'll learn more about the decision-making process in the next chapter. In the meantime, know that practicing abstinence is not always an easy decision to make, but it's often a responsible one.

Adolescent Development

Adolescence is a time of life defined by change. Suddenly you're no longer a child. You're beginning to view the world differently, in a more sophisticated way. You are now capable of understanding abstract concepts. Whereas just a few years ago you were able to think of things only in very limited terms, you can now reason logically. In addition, you are more capable now of seeing things from another person's perspective—not only from your own.

Some of the most dramatic changes you experience when you become a teenager are the physical ones. Your body is now producing hormones, chemical messengers within your system that cause the maturing of certain organs. This stage of human development is known as puberty, and it's during this phase that you will become capable of bearing children.

As mentioned in Chapter 1, during puberty boys' testes begin to produce sperm, and girls begin having menstrual periods. The hormones that cause these physical changes— testosterone for boys and progesterone and estrogen for girls—are known as sex hormones, and they cause emotional changes as well as physical ones. Awareness of sexual feelings and desires is a completely normal part of adolescence, although different people feel them at different times and in different ways. Sometimes people feel excited, thrilled, or delighted by their sexual feelings. Sometimes they feel upset, scared, ashamed, angry, or guilty. Sometimes they feel a combination of feelings. And sometimes sexual feelings can be overwhelming. Sexual feelings offer you a choice: Do you or don't you want to act on them?

Finding satisfying and healthy outlets for sexual feelings is an important part of being a sexual person, and that will be discussed more fully later in this chapter. In the meantime, it's important to know that according to studies from the U.S. Department of Health and Human Services and from the Alan Guttmacher Institute, the more hobbies a teenager becomes involved in, the less likely he or she is to become sexually active at a young age.

Pressure to Say Yes

Rob never told Tess this, but the truth is that the first time he had sex, he was scared, shy, and so nervous that he can barely remember enjoying it at all. If Rob's friends had been different, chances are he wouldn't have had sex that time at all. But Rob's friends were already comparing notes on sex—talking about their experiences, laughing about different girls—and Rob didn't want to feel left out. Even worse, he didn't want the guys to think he wasn't man enough to do it. Even before his first experience, he had begun to lie about how much he had done, just to keep up with the conversation.

Peer pressure is as big a part of the teenage years as the physical changes described above. Sometimes pressure can actually be helpful. Members of a basketball or football team, for example, can sometimes motivate each other to work harder during practice and excel to a greater extent on the playing field.

But peer pressure can also be quite damaging. When friends encourage each other to do drugs or drink alcohol, for example, that can have dangerous short-term consequences, such as accidents on the road, as well as long-term ones, such as physical and emotional addiction. Similarly, pressure from peers—whether it's someone you're going out with or people you're just friends with—to become sexually active can be very damaging: It can encourage someone to begin a sexual relationship before he or she is ready to. A person who is sexually active puts him or herself at risk not only of pregnancy, but of contracting a sexually transmitted disease, such as syphilis, chlamydia, herpes, or AIDS. (For more information, contact one of the agencies listed on page 128–129.)

How to Say No

It may be hard to resist peer pressure—but it's certainly easy to tell someone else to do it! Do these words sound familiar?: "Just say no—it's easy." "If they don't like you for the decision you make, they weren't your friends to begin with." By now, you've probably heard them all.

The truth is, it *isn't* easy to say no to something when all your friends are doing it. The stakes are high—do something, or you may lose a friend, or your romance may end, or you may be laughed at the next day. Everyone's been there, and no one's ever had it easy.

Resisting pressure requires good communication skills. It requires stamina and willpower. And it requires confidence that what you're doing is right for you, even though it may not be right for others. Finally, resisting pressure requires high self-esteem. Tess is one high school student who had low self-esteem. Deep down, she always thought of herself as ugly and kind of uncool. What made her feel best about herself was the fact that Rob liked her. So when it came down to the choice of sleeping with Rob or risking his rejection, Tess didn't have the confidence to say no.

Raising Self-Esteem

How high is your self-esteem? Try taking this test* and rating it yourself.

1) When you get up in the morning and look at yourself in the mirror, what do you say?
   a. "I look great this morning! And I'm about to have a great day."
   b. "Oh, no, not you again! Why do I even bother to get out of bed?"
2) When you fail at something or make a big mistake, what do you tell yourself?
   a. "Everyone has the right to fail or make mistakes every day."
   b. "I blew it again! I can't do anything right! I should have known better."
3) When you succeed at something, what do you say to yourself?
   a. "Congratulations! I should be proud of myself."
   b. "I could have done better, if I had tried harder."
4) You have just talked to someone who has power or authority in your life, a parent, teacher, a member of the clergy, or coach. What do you tell yourself?
   a. "I handled that pretty well."
   b. "I acted so stupid! I always say dumb things."
5) You have just left the first meeting of a club you joined. What do you say to yourself?
   a. "That was fun. I met some new people I liked."
   b. "I talked too much, and nobody liked me. Everybody hated my joke."

---

6) You have just left a friend's house. What do you tell yourself?

   a. "That was fun. My friend really likes me."

   b. "My friend was just pretending to like me. I probably won't get invited back ever again."

7) When someone gives you a compliment or says, "I like you," what do you say to yourself?

   a. "I deserve it!"

   b. "Nobody gives me a compliment unless they want something back. Besides, I don't deserve it."

8) When someone you care about lets you down, what do you tell yourself?

   a. "My feelings are hurt, but I'll get over it. Later I can try to find out what happened."

   b. "This proves that that person doesn't care about me."

9) When you let down someone you care about, what do you say to yourself?

   a. "It isn't nice, and it isn't fun, but sometimes people let each other down. I admit to what I did; now I'll get on with my life."

   b. "How could I do such a terrible thing? I should be ashamed of myself."

10) When you feel needy or unsure of yourself, what do you tell yourself?

   a. "Everyone feels this way sometimes. I'll feel better soon."

   b. "Grow up—don't be such a baby. Just deal with it."

Scoring: Give yourself 10 points for every (a) answer and 5 points for every (b) answer. Then use the following key to find out your self-esteem.

Key:

90–100: Your self-esteem is high and positive.

75–90: Your self-esteem could be better.

60–75: Be kinder to yourself. Remember that you're only human.
50–60: You don't give yourself nearly enough credit for your good points, and you're way too hard on yourself for your mistakes. Luckily, there are things you can do to have a more realistic view of yourself.

How did you do? If you, like most of us, could stand to feel better about yourself, here are some things you might try.

1) Be easier on yourself. Yes, you're human. Everyone else is, too. Keep in mind that you are much more aware of what you consider to be your shortcomings than are other people, who are usually too busy thinking about their own weaknesses to pay much attention to yours.

2) Treat yourself well. When you talk to yourself, what kinds of things do you say? If you find yourself thinking things like "I'm really stupid" or "I'm such a jerk," you might want to change your internal language. Start giving yourself credit for the things you do well. If you did a good job on a project, for example, take time to talk to yourself positively. Go ahead and admit it—tell yourself that you did a great job and that you deserve the praise you're getting.

3) Be good at something. And speaking of your achievements, try to concentrate on the things you excel at. Chances are you'll find that the list is long. Maybe what you're good at is something obvious, like being a good student or a gifted athlete. Maybe your talents are more subtle, like being a good friend or knowing how to listen —two very valuable gifts. Maybe your greatest talent— or the thing you enjoy doing the most—is something uncommon, like walking on stilts. Every human being has something to be proud of. What are your open or hidden gifts?

4) Take responsibility for your actions. We all have a difficult time recognizing and admitting that we've done something wrong, but it's especially hard when you're already down on yourself. Even so, knowing when you are to blame for something and having the courage to admit it, can actually make you feel better about yourself —prouder and more secure. To know that you were able to come forward and accept responsibility for a mistake you made can really improve your feelings toward yourself.

5) Find a support group. Many people find upsetting things easier to deal with if they have a friend or a group of friends to talk to. A support group—three or more friends who can talk honestly and openly with each other—also makes the good things that happen to you more joyful, because you have people to share them with. Think for a moment about people whom you can trust, friends whom you can be honest with, and who are honest with you. Friends like these are not easy to come by, and you may only be able to think of one or two. But even a support group that consists of two friends can do wonders for the way you feel about yourself and each other.

6) Learn how to say no. It might take some practice, but if other people are doing something that you don't want to do or that you feel is wrong, try turning down their requests that you join them. You may be surprised at how good it makes you feel about yourself.

7) Be true to yourself and others. People who feel good about themselves have the courage to act with honesty and integrity. This means knowing when to put others first and having the confidence not to take credit for the achievements of other people. If you take the time to thank friends or acquaintances for something they've done for you or to recognize a job they've done well, you'll find that people will respect your unselfishness and that your self-esteem will soar.

Effective Communication

Tonya remembers how upset she was when she and Jack didn't agree about "this whole sex thing," as Tonya called it. What troubled Tonya almost as much as the issue itself was the fact that she and Jack weren't communicating at all about it. They were arguing all the time, but neither could see the other's point of view. And for that reason, the issue had come between them.

Then one day, Tonya's health teacher spent an entire class discussing the importance of effective communication skills. Tonya found herself leaning forward and listening to every word. When she got home that night, she spent a whole hour reviewing those skills and thinking about how to use them to talk to Jack.

The confidence you have in yourself is often reflected in the way you speak and listen to other people. For that reason, effective communication may be the most important part of resisting peer pressure. If you let a person know you are not interested in doing something in a clear and straightforward manner, chances are you will keep the other person's respect. More important, you will keep the respect you have for yourself.

It may not seem enough to have a person *respect* you when what you really want is for that person to *like* you, and to want to *be* with you. The truth is, though, that if you do something you don't want to do in order to keep someone's friendship or affection, it often catches up with you. It may sound old-fashioned, but you could end up liking yourself less for doing something you think is wrong to please another person. The choice, of course, is up to you.

Here are some basic rules of effective communication.

1) Using "I" messages. People who disagree strongly about an issue don't always know how to communicate their differences of opinion to one another. Sometimes they

end up becoming hurt, insulted, and even angrier than they were before the discussion began. One way to cut down on unnecessary insults is to communicate through "I" messages instead of "you" messages.

Here's an example. Let's say you want to go to a party Saturday night, but your friend Terry wants to go to the movies instead. The two of you have been talking all week about what you want to do, but you can't agree, and you're both becoming impatient. You're beginning to feel as though Terry is either too shy to go to a social event or is embarrassed to be seen with you in public.

A "you" message to Terry would be something like this: "Why don't you want to go to the party with me? Are you ashamed of me?"

An "I" message, on the other hand, puts the same information in terms of the person who's speaking, not the person being spoken to: "Sometimes I get the feeling you're embarrassed to be with me in public. I'm not sure if you mean it that way, but I have to tell you that it hurts my feelings."

There is an important difference between these two messages. In the first example, the word "I" is not used. Terry, as a result, may feel accused of something and is likely to become defensive. The second message focuses on the speaker's feelings, which makes this example seem much less accusing than the first. For that reason, Terry is much more likely to discuss the issue at hand than to argue it.

2) Communicating without words. Not every form of communication requires talking. You can often tell how a person feels about something by watching his or her body language. In general, people who feel strongly about something and have confidence in what they are feeling are able to look the other person squarely in the eye as they are speaking and listening. People who are less sure of themselves may turn their eyes away and

look elsewhere. Tonya realized that every time she talked to Jack about not being ready to have sex with him, she would have to look directly at him to underline her feelings.

Next time you have a disagreement with someone, think about the message you're giving to the other person. Are you leaning forward, showing that you're engaged in the conversation, or are you slumped in your chair, indicating boredom or a lack of interest? Are you using your hands to gesture as a way to emphasize what you're saying, or are you fiddling with your hair or your clothes, which may make you look nervous? Keep in mind when you are talking about something that matters to you that the things you do with your body say as much to the other person as the words that come out of your mouth.

3) Listening. Effective communication requires more than just speaking. Listening is equally important. The best way to show a person you're talking to that you hear what he or she is saying is to practice "active listening." This type of listening can be as challenging as speaking well, sometimes even more so. Here are some guidelines you can follow to make yourself a better, more active listener.

- Pay full attention to the speaker. Concentrate on what the other person is saying—don't let your attention wander.

- Look at a person when you're listening, just as when you are speaking. Looking is a sign that you are giving the speaker your full attention.

- Provide the speaker with your own ideas about what he or she is talking about. This type of participation shows the speaker that you are interested in what is being said.

- Don't interrupt. As eager as you may be to participate in the conversation, don't forget that you are listening to someone. Wait until the speaker has finished a sentence or thought before jumping in with your own thoughts.

For example, Tonya knew she'd have to listen to Jack's point of view about sexual intimacy patiently and actively. She realized that if she didn't, there was little chance that Jack would sit and listen to hers.

4) Resolving Conflicts. Even if you practice all the steps required for effective communication, conflicts may still arise, particularly if you are talking about something as volatile as whether or not to become sexually intimate. Knowing how to minimize these conflicts and how to resolve them peacefully is a vital skill that will not only help you resist peer pressure resistance but will also help you communicate better in all aspects of life.

Many health classes teach students that conflict resolution is a seven-step process known as RESPECT*. This word not only emphasizes the regard and kindness people should treat each other with—regardless of the subject of their disagreement—but it helps remind them of a specific strategy.

- **R**ecognize that the two of you disagree.
- **E**liminate the need to emphasize what your opinion is for the time being. You can save that for later.
- **S**can (or review) and listen to the other person's opinion. This means to focus closely on the basic points the other person is making, using the active listening skills described above.
- **P**araphrase the information the person is giving you. To paraphrase is to put something in your own words. By paraphrasing, you are sharing with the other person your own thoughts about the conversation and showing that you are listening to him or her.
- **E**xpress your opinion. Now is your turn to be heard, but be sure to do it calmly, stating the reasons you want what you're asking for.

---

*Used with permission from *Holt Health*, by Jerrold Greenberg and Robert Gold, © 1999 by Holt, Rinehart and Winston.

- *C*ompromise. Sometimes this is difficult to do, especially when it comes to something as important as sexual intimacy. But it is possible for two people to reach an agreement and an alternative solution if they care enough about one another.
- *T*ry to live with the compromise. Again, it's not easy. But this is in many ways the most important step of the process. And if the first solution doesn't work, another one may.

Tonya reviewed all her notes carefully. She understood that she'd have to practice all the things she had learned that day in order to get anywhere with Jack. She didn't think she'd have much of a problem with the effective communication skills, although she knew that at times she was a better talker than listener. What worried her the most was the compromise part of the RESPECT process for resolving conflict. How could she compromise with Jack, when she knew he wanted to have sex and she didn't? What if Jack told her that if she didn't sleep with him he'd break up with her? What if she broke down?

Tonya finally decided that her compromise would be telling Jack that she'd be willing to let him see other people, and if he decided at that point that he'd rather be with someone else than with her, she'd understand. They had a conversation, and it wasn't an easy one. Here's how it went.

Tonya: You know if you feel that strongly about sleeping with someone, and the truth is that I'm not ready to sleep with anyone yet—even you—I have to tell you that you might want to think about going out with other people. And if you meet someone who you'd rather be with, I'll understand, and get out of your way so you can do that.

Jack: What's that supposed to mean? You want me to find someone else to sleep with instead of you? What's going on with you?

Tonya: No, no. I'm not saying this because I want you to—I really want you *not* to. It would be so hard for me if you left me for someone else. But I don't want to feel like I'm holding you to this relationship—you know, without sex, if you're dying to sleep with someone. So I kind of feel like I need to give you the option to break up with me and see other people.

Jack: I don't get you. What am I supposed to say?

Tonya: I'm doing this because . . .

Jack: You need to know that I don't want to sleep with just anyone—I want to sleep with *you.*

Tonya: That means a lot to me. But you need to know that the option is there for you.

Making the decision to let Jack see other people was really hard for Tonya, but it was the only way she could think to compromise with him. And as it turned out, he never did ask anyone else out.

Resisting Peer Pressure

Now that you're familiar with the skills you need for effective communication, it's time to see how you could apply them in order to resist peer pressure. Let's say a boyfriend or girlfriend is pressuring you to have sex with him or her. Here are some methods you can use to help you say no.

Verbal Pressure Resistance
The most obvious way to resist pressure is to say no. Uttering that one word can be very effective in certain situations, but if you're not comfortable doing that, there is

a process you can follow that may make it easier. This five-step process gives you time to present your side to the other person and also allows you to take some control of the situation.

1) State what you're being pressured to do. In this case, the person you're involved with wants to have sex with you.
2) State what you want to do. Now is the time to say that you don't want to—or are not ready to—have sexual intercourse.
3) State what you would like to do instead. Here you can say that you care about the person and that you'd like to continue seeing him or her—but only without pressure to have sex.
4) State what can happen if your conditions are met. You can talk here about the great relationship that the two of you have, and remind the person that there are so many other things the two of you can share.
5) State what can happen if your conditions are not met. Here's the hard part. Saying no always involves a risk, and here is where you need to put things on the line. You need to tell the other person that if the pressure to have sexual intercourse does not end, you will have to end the relationship.

Keep in mind that taking a risk such as the one outlined in Step 5 almost always has a reward. Even if your relationship ends, you'll always know that you took control of a difficult situation, which not only will make you feel better about yourself but will probably win your ex boy- or girlfriend's respect, even if he or she doesn't admit it.

Nonverbal Pressure Resistance

As we saw earlier, body language is an important part of effective communication. It plays just as significant a role in resisting pressure. If you look a person straight in the eye when you state how you feel about not having sex yet, it will reflect your own confidence and self-respect. If, on the other hand, you look at the floor, play with your hair or nails, or fold your arms, you may be seen as being unsure of yourself, regardless of the strength of your words.

Asserting Your Message

As convincing as you may sound and look, you may not be heard the first time around. It could be that your boyfriend or girlfriend doesn't want to believe that you'd actually end the relationship rather than have sexual intercourse. He or she may stop pressuring you for the time being and then begin again a few days later. You might have to remind him or her of your stand. Should this be the case, here are two strategies you might use.

1) Say it again. Everytime you're pressured, repeat your conditions. Try to boil your point down to two or better yet, one, sentence: "I just don't want to have sex yet, and I want the pressure to end." You may sound like a broken record, but eventually you will be heard.

2) Separate the issues. Let's say the person you're involved with says, "If you really loved me, you'd sleep with me." There are really two separate issues. If you tell your boyfriend or girlfriend that you really do love him or her, which is why the two of you are going out and spend so much time together, the first part of the complaint will be taken care of. You can even say that if you didn't love him or her, you wouldn't take the time to talk about this whole issue—you'd just end the relationship. Regarding the second part, you could say that sexual intercourse is something you're just not ready for and that there are a lot other things people who are in love can do together.

Practicing Your Message

Although Tonya had a number of friends she was close to, she didn't feel she could talk to any of them about this. Most of them had already had sex, and they just wouldn't understand why Tonya was hesitating. And Tonya's older sister and parents were out of the question, too. "You're only 15," they'd say. "What is wrong with Jack for even trying to push you?"

Tonya decided to write down things Jack would say to her and to come up with possible responses herself before actually talking to him. What Tonya chose to do was to role-play her situation. Role-playing is an excellent exercise if you are practicing saying no to someone who is pressuring you.

Tonya knew Jack well enough to imagine the kinds of things he'd probably say to her. She wrote down what he'd say and then wrote down what she would say in response.

Jack: Oh, come on, Tonya, we love each other, right? Having sex is what people do when they love each other.

Tonya: People who love each other also wait until the time is right for both of them before they go ahead and have sex. If one person pressures the other, that's not really love.

Jack: You know, everyone's doing it. Any other girl would say yes.

Tonya: If it means that little to you, go ahead and ask any other girl. She's not going to love you the way I do.

Jack: Look, why don't we try it once. If you hate it, we won't do it again, I promise.

Tonya: That's not good enough—I'm not ready to do it, whether it's once or ten times.

Physical Pressure and Resistance

Not all types of pressure are verbal. Sometimes people who want to have sexual intercourse can become physical and overpowering. If you're uncomfortable going out with someone because he (girls are physically pressured more often than boys are) has become physical with you in a way that you have not liked, and if you don't feel that he's listened when you've said no, then no matter how high your self-esteem and how sharp your communication techniques are, it might be dangerous to go out with him again.

Physical pressures leaves no room for negotiation. If you are out with someone who physically pressures you to do something against your will, you need to try to get away as quickly as possible. Run away if you can, and if you have to use physical force of your own in order to do so that is entirely appropriate. In addition, know that no matter what was said or done that led up to the assault, it was not your fault that it happened. The responsibility for physical pressure (or rape, which sometimes results) is always with the assailant, never with the victim. There are people you can talk to if you think you've been forced to do something against your will. Rape crisis centers are listed in the yellow pages of most phone books. See Chapter 7 and *Straight Talk About Date Rape* for more information.

Alternatives

As mentioned earlier in this chapter, studies show that the more hobbies teenagers have, the less likely they are to become sexually active at an early age. What are your favorite activities? Do you love sports? Is music more your thing? How about getting involved in community causes, such as working in a soup kitchen or volunteering in a nursing home?

You've probably heard this before. Oh great, you might be thinking. Another book telling me to ride my bike or to take a guitar lesson instead of having sex with my girl-friend/boyfriend. It may sound clichéd, but there really are a lot of activities and causes around that you can concen-trate your energy and intelligence on. Sexual activity is most definitely not the only alternative to boredom.

Activities for Two

In a similar vein, not every single date has to lead to situations where sex seems like the only logical conclusion. Instead of curling up every Friday night with a rented movie, popcorn, and one another, it may be a good idea to go out for pizza, see more movies in theaters, and go to ball games. In fact, when Tonya talked to Jack about her feelings about sex, one of the compromises she offered to make was to go to more basketball games with him. She knew it was Jack's favorite sport not only to play but to watch, and she thought it would be a good way for them to spend time together in a less intimate atmosphere. And in spite of herself—Tonya was not much of a sports fan—she found herself following the games closely and enjoying them thoroughly.

If you're seeing someone who is constantly pushing for intimate time alone with you, you may want to suggest to him or her that together you do some things with friends or in more social settings. Sometimes it can be stifling to be alone with each other all evening long. Group activities are usually less likely to lead to uncomfortable situations, and they can be another way to have fun besides romantic, intimate dates.

Jack and Tonya did a lot of talking. It wasn't easy, but Tonya got Jack to see where she was coming from. The hardest part for Tonya were the compromises she felt she should give Jack as part of the conflict resolution process she had learned in class. She told Jack that if he needed to see other people to figure out how he felt about things, he should go ahead and do that—she'd give him the freedom. She was happy to hear Jack say that he didn't want to see anyone else.

For his part, Jack found himself loving Tonya's sense of self-respect. Rather than being turned off by her refusal to sleep with him—as some of his friends would have been —he became attracted to her in a completely new way. He wanted to find out how she felt about other things—her family, her schoolwork, the movies they saw—and he wanted to talk to her about the things he was going through, too. In a funny way, the whole issue of whether to have sex brought Tonya and Jack closer together. They ended up becoming even closer friends than they were before.

3

Responsible
Sexual Behavior

Ever since Valerie and Trey started seeing each other four weeks ago, it's all they can do to keep from kissing all the time—in class, at the movies, on the street. Trey thinks about Valerie all the time—at night, in the morning, in math class, during basketball practice. He also thinks all the time about having sex with her. He's wanted to from the moment he saw her in class this year. They haven't done it yet, but Trey figures they will this weekend. They're going to be alone—Trey's folks are out of town, and Valerie has told her mom that she's spending the night with her friend Jess.

Trey's done everything right. The dinner was incredible, especially with the red wine he'd managed to snatch from his parents' liquor cabinet. The music on the stereo is romantic, and he and Valerie are on the sofa, kissing and touching. Trey knows the time is right. He takes Valerie by the hand and leads her into his room.

Trey doesn't know how nervous Valerie is. She'd never done this before and hasn't had the nerve to tell Trey. What if it hurts? What if she's bad at it? What if Trey doesn't want to have anything to do with her the next day? And wait a minute—what about pregnancy? Shouldn't they be using something?

The last thing on Trey's mind is pregnancy. Maybe if Valerie had said something, he would have found a condom to use, but she didn't, and there's no turning back. The next morning Trey is unbelievably happy. He tells Valerie he loves her and that he wants to be with her all the time.

Two months go by, and time is flying for Trey and Valerie both. Sex is getting to be more and more fun. Valerie loves the way it makes her feel: so grown up and so loved. Trey uses condoms when Valerie asks him to, but she doesn't like asking him. She worries that bringing up birth control will kill the romantic mood, and neither one of them likes the way condoms feel. And anyway, Valerie hasn't gotten pregnant. Maybe they'll just keep being lucky.

Three years have passed since Tonya and Jack had their talk about abstinence. And Jack has kept his word—he hasn't pressured her about it at all. But that doesn't mean they never talk about it—actually, they often talk about their feelings, about their future, and about when the right time is to have sex.

Lately Tonya has found herself wondering, is the right time now? She's certain that she's in love with Jack and that he feels the same way about her. She *feels* ready to have sex, but how can she know for sure? She decides to talk to her older sister, Maria, who's been married for five years.

When Tonya tells Maria why she wants to talk to her, Maria suggests that her friend Lucy, whom Tonya's known for a long time, should be there too. Tonya likes Lucy a lot; she feels comfortable talking to Lucy, so she agrees.

Tonya tells Maria and Lucy that she's ready to have sex with Jack. They're in love with each other, they're together all the time, and she still worries at times that if she doesn't have sex with him soon, she may lose him. Maria interrupts her. "If you feel like you're going to lose him if you don't sleep with him, that's not a good enough reason," she says. "If he's pressuring you, you need to forget about it."

Tonya thinks about this. She realizes Jack isn't the one who's doing the pushing. "I think the pressure is coming from me, not from Jack," she says.

Making a Responsible Decision

It's completely normal to feel internal pressure to have sex—"Everyone else is doing it; shouldn't I be doing it too?"—and to desire or want it, as well. It's also normal to have doubts and second thoughts about sex. In fact, these concerns should be taken seriously. Think for a moment about Valerie and Trey and about Jack and Tonya. Which couple is behaving more responsibly?

As you learned in the last chapter, the only certain way to avoid becoming pregnant is to delay sexual intercourse. The fact is, however, that by the time most teenagers are old enough to finish high school, they have become sexually intimate with someone. According to a 1996 study by the U.S. Department of Health and Human Services, slightly more than half of females and nearly two-thirds of males have had intercourse by their 18th birthday. That rate has risen steadily, doubling since the mid-1980s, which is one explanation for the rise in teen birth rates—they're nearly one-quarter higher in 1996 than they were in 1986.

But pregnancy and sexually transmitted diseases are not the only risks involved with sexual intercourse. There are emotional risks as well. That's why the decision of whether to have sex—and when and how to have it—is such an important one.

The Decision-Making Process

When was the last time you had to make a decision? Chances are, you face them almost every day. Some decisions are tougher to make than others are. It's definitely easier, for example, to choose what you want to eat for breakfast than it is to decide whether or not to refuse alcohol at a party when everyone else is drinking, or whether or not to go with a group of friends to a movie when you have a math test the next day. People can tell you what they think you should do in these cases, but to make the choice that's right for you—and to stick to it—requires more than someone telling you how to behave. It requires you and your feelings about yourself and the situation.

Fortunately there is a process you can follow that can help you with difficult decisions. Many health books call this the "decision-making process," and it involves four steps.

1) Consider your options.
2) Think about the benefits and consequences of those options.
3) Consider your values.
4) Weigh your options in light of your values, and make your decision.

Let's say that, like Tonya, you're thinking about having sex with a boyfriend or girlfriend. Here's how the decision-making process can help you make your choice.

1) Consider your options. The choice you're facing is the same one Tonya is thinking about. It's the decision Valerie had to make during her evening with Trey, and the one that millions of teenagers face every year. You can practice abstinence, or you can have sexual intercourse.
2) Think about the benefits and consequences of those options. Here's where things get more complicated.

Every relationship has its own set of circumstances and its own patterns.

There are many benefits to practicing abstinence. For one thing, it's the safest way to ensure that a pregnancy will not occur and that neither partner will contract a sexually transmitted disease. In addition, contrary to what a lot of people think, delaying sexual intercourse often makes a relationship more intimate. Abstinence is a mutual decision made out of trust and commitment. It's a signal that a relationship does not have to be sexual in order to be fulfilling. Tonya and Jack are close friends as well as potential sexual partners. This is a benefit that often occurs between two people who choose to delay sexual intercourse.

On the other hand, practicing abstinence can have a major consequence: It could jeopardize a relationship. This is particularly true if one person wants to have sexual intercourse and the other one does not. Valerie, for example, probably would have preferred it if she could have delayed sexual intercourse with Trey until she felt more comfortable. She was worried, however, that Trey would not continue to go out with her if she didn't sleep with him. For Valerie, the negative consequences of abstinence outweighed the benefits.

Tonya, as opposed to Valerie, has always felt strongly that there were more advantages than disadvantages to abstinence. But recently she has begun to consider the benefits of sexual intercourse. When sex occurs between two mature people who love, respect, and trust one another, it can be an extremely rewarding experience. Tonya feels that she and Jack have that type of relationship and that she's ready to express her love for him in a more physical way.

At the same time, Maria and Lucy remind Tonya that sexual intercourse has its own set of possible consequences. In the first place, it can cause a pregnancy. When used responsibly, birth control can lower the chances of a pregnancy occurring, but no method is foolproof.

Sexually transmitted diseases (STDs) are another possible consequence of sexual intercourse. According to the Centers for Disease Control, more than 100,000 teenagers contracted a sexually transmitted disease in 1995. The most dangerous type of STD is AIDS, but there are others—somewhat less dangerous but far more common—such as syphilis, chlamydia, gonorrhea, and herpes.

Sexual intercourse has emotional consequences as well. Two people who are involved in a sexual relationship make a commitment to one another. When that commitment is broken, the results can be very painful. For example, Valerie was very relieved when Trey told her his feelings the morning after their night together. Had Trey ignored her or broken up with her, she would have suffered much more than she would have if they *hadn't* slept together. Sexual intercourse is an intimate act that can leave a person extremely vulnerable.

3. Consider your values. Think about the things that matter most to you. What qualities do you look for in a friend or in someone you confide in? Your values may not be easy to define, but they're very important to consider when you're making a difficult choice. If you are contemplating a decision that goes against the values you have, it may be a good idea to reconsider. Tonya, for example, has always believed that sex outside of marriage is wrong. She worries that having intercourse with Jack will conflict with that particular priority. Here are some other values that Tonya thinks are important:
   • honesty
   • trustworthiness
   • responsibility
   • respect for herself and others
   • compassion
   • self-control
   • a sense of social justice

Take some time to make your own list of values. Some values may be widely agreed upon, such as the values of a particular religion or the idea that killing people is generally wrong. Some values are personal—everyone has his or her own list. Whatever your values, the decisions you make should always be consistent with the priorities you set for yourself.

4) Weigh your options in light of your values, and make your decision. Many people think this is the easy part of making a choice. You've thought through everything, you've considered your values, the rest should be easy, right? Actually, it's not.

This fourth step is the crucial one. Keep in mind that the choices you make are up to you, and not to anyone else. Important decisions, such as whether to have sexual intercourse, usually require time, patience, and a great deal of thought. And regardless of what decision you end up making, there is still a risk involved. There are never any guarantees when it comes to difficult choices. But the decision-making model can help you lower the risks while preparing you for the benefits and consequences of the course of action you end up taking.

The Keys to a Responsible Relationship

The decisions you make are an important facet of responsible behavior, but there are aspects to responsibility. This is particularly true if you are romantically involved with someone. Anyone who's ever been in a relationship— whether with a friend, a family member, or a romantic partner—can tell you that it takes a great deal of effort in order for it to be successful.

In a romantic relationship the work doesn't end once a couple begins having sexual intercourse. In fact, once a relationship becomes sexual, it becomes more important than ever for both people involved to keep thinking about their feelings and talking to each other.

Trey has noticed, for example, that he and Valerie don't really talk very much anymore. When they have a conversation, it's usually about where they can go for their next sexual encounter. Trey's glad that they're having sex, but in a weird way it's as if that's all Valerie thinks about now. He misses the jokes and chatter they used to have. He mentions this to Valerie one day. "Come on, big guy," Valerie says, "we always talk and have a great time, whenever we're in bed."

Jack has done a lot of talking and thinking about his relationship with Tonya. He knows he's ready for sexual intercourse, but he doesn't want to mess things up with her. He's aware that she doesn't believe in sex before marriage—and what if he gets her pregnant? On the other hand, all his friends are having sex. They think Jack's concerns are pretty stupid—why can't he and Tonya stop thinking, and just do it?

Emotional Maturity

Actually, Jack's concerns aren't stupid at all; in fact, they're a sign of maturity. Emotional maturity is very important to any relationship but is especially crucial when sex is involved. Many people associate the word *maturity* with age. It's true that the older you are, the more time you have had to become mature. But many people in their 50s and 60s are not emotionally mature, while some teenagers, like Jack, are already emotionally mature.

What determines a person's maturity? Here are some of the factors.

Honesty: It's not as easy as it sounds. Being honest can be difficult and even painful. But without it, a relationship is almost certain to fail.

The ability to compromise: Knowing how to compromise requires more than letting your partner choose the movie you're going to see on Saturday night. It means seeing a situation from more than one point of view and sometimes putting another person's needs in front of your own.

Effective communication: As you learned in Chapter 2, good communication involves more than just talking. It's equally important to know how to listen. And since every relationship has its share of disagreements, knowing how to resolve conflicts quickly and effectively is part of good communication—as well as being another characteristic of emotional maturity. Here's a quick review of some of the keys to effective communication discussed in Chapter 2.

- **Use "I" messages instead of "you" messages.** If you have had a disagreement and need to talk about it, keep in mind that it's always better to use sentences that have "I" in them because they are less accusatory and more open to negotiation. For example, if your boy- or girl-friend didn't call you when he or she had promised to, it's better to say "I expected you to call and was hurt when you didn't" than "You were supposed to call me and you didn't."
- **Communicate without words.** Remember that when you are talking to someone your body language can speak as loudly as your words. Look your boy- or girlfriend straight in the eye. Lean forward in your chair while listening, instead of slumping in it. That way you will look as though the conversation is an important one that interests you.
- **Practice active listening.** Pay full attention when your boy- or girlfriend is talking. Don't interrupt, but be sure to ask questions or provide feedback so that he or she will know you are interested in what is being said.
- **Try to resolve conflicts peacefully.** The RESPECT guidelines discussed on pages 36–37 can help you do this.

Like all skills, effective communication requires dedication and a great deal of practice. Tonya and Jack know this; they've had their share of conversations, disagreements, and arguments. Fortunately, they've always been able to work their problems out. Valerie and Trey haven't ever really argued, but they haven't been together for very long.

Sexual Intimacy vs. Emotional Intimacy: Knowing the Difference

The word *intimate* has a lot of different meanings. Being intimate with someone could mean being close to him or her emotionally. It could mean sharing food, gossip, jokes, and secrets. It could mean arguing about something for hours and then laughing about it a few days later. People who are intimate with each other in this way usually care for, respect, and trust one another. Those are the three keystones to what is called "emotional intimacy."

Another way to be intimate with someone is through something called "sexual intimacy." This type of closeness is easier to define. Health textbooks and other reference sources usually define "sexual intimacy" as touching another person's breasts and genitals. This type of intimacy is physical, although it may also be emotional.

Many relationships feature both types of intimacy. And it sometimes happens that people get the two types of intimacy mixed up. Sometimes a couple who were emotionally intimate lose some of that intimacy when the relationship becomes sexual as well. On the other hand, some couples find that they become closer emotionally once they become sexually intimate. And of course, some couples are more intimate in one way than in the other. How would you define the intimacy between Jack and Tonya, and the intimacy between Trey and Valerie?

High Self-Esteem

Being in a responsible sexual relationship also requires having high self-esteem. Chapter 2 stressed that high self-esteem is a valuable characteristic to have if you are choosing to abstain from sexual intercourse. In some ways, it's a quality that's even more important if you are in a sexual relationship. Having a relationship of any kind means compromising, sharing, and negotiating. When sex is part of that relationship, the stakes can become higher because so many emotions are involved. The healthiest sexual relationships are usually between two people who have enough confidence not only in one another but in themselves to talk things over honestly and effectively.

Let's review here the steps involved in raising one's self-esteem, which were discussed in Chapter 2.

1) Be easier on yourself. Don't blame yourself for everything, if and when things go wrong.
2) Treat yourself well. If your boyfriend or girlfriend breaks up with you, try to look at it as his or her loss, not yours.
3) Be good at something. Remember that there are things that define you—things you are proud of, such as sports, music, or art—other than the relationship.
4) Take responsibility for your actions. If you have a disagreement with your boy- or girlfriend, apologize if you think you were in the wrong. It will make you feel better and is always good for the relationship as well.
5) Find a support group. Even if you are in love, you will always need friends, families, or trusted adults to lend perspective not only (and not always) to your relationship but to life itself.

More Essential Qualities

Being emotionally intimate with someone is an important part of being in a responsible and healthy sexual relationship. So is being mature, honest, trustworthy, compassionate, and communicative with each other. In addition to these priorities, responsible sexual behavior requires using contraceptives consistently and correctly. You'll learn more about that later in the chapter.

There are also other essential qualities to a responsible sexual relationship. Here are a few.

Mutual consent: Sexual intercourse should occur only if both partners involved are willing.

Equality: People who are having a sexual relationship should treat each other with an equal amount of kindness, fairness, and respect.

Attentiveness: It's especially important for people who share sexual intimacy to talk and listen to one another not only during a sexual encounter but at other times, too.

Mutual protection from physical and emotional harm: It is up to both people who are in a sexual relationship to protect themselves and each other emotionally. In short, this means being kind to and about each another. In addition, both partners are equally responsible for taking measures to prevent sexually transmitted diseases and for using contraceptives correctly in order to minimize the risk of pregnancy.

Sexual Intimacy

It's important to know that being sexually intimate with someone does not necessarily mean having sexual intercourse with that person. You should also be aware that there are actually three different kinds of sexual intercourse. The first, vaginal intercourse, occurs when a man's penis enters a woman's vagina. This type of intercourse is what causes pregnancy. It can also leave both partners at risk of contracting sexually transmitted diseases, including AIDS. The second type of sexual intercourse is oral intercourse, which refers to contact between one person's mouth and another person's genitals. A person can't get pregnant from having oral intercourse (also called oral sex). It does, however, involve an exchange of bodily fluids (semen, blood, and/or saliva), which means that people who engage in oral intercourse can be at risk of contracting a sexually transmitted disease. The third type of sexual intercourse is anal intercourse, which happens when a man's penis enters another person's anus. Again, anal intercourse does not lead to pregnancy. It can, however, leave a person at risk of contracting a sexually transmitted disease, particularly AIDS, again because people engaging in anal intercourse do exchange bodily fluids.

Options to Intercourse

Two people who want to be sexually intimate with each other do not necessarily have to risk pregnancy or sexually transmitted diseases in order to do so. There are other methods that can help a person feel sexually satisfied. These methods are sometimes called "sexual outercourse," because they are behaviors that do not involve penetration (either vaginal, oral, or anal) and do not involve an exchange of bodily fluids.

These methods include masturbation, which is the stimulation of one's own—or a partner's—genitals, and phone sex, which is the sharing of sexual fantasy over the phone (sometimes accompanied by mutual masturbation). Two people can also share erotic fantasies with each other in person; take showers or baths with each other; or engage in kissing and petting, which means caressing each another. On the whole, sexual outercourse is a safer behavior than sexual intercourse because when done properly, there is no risk of pregnancy or sexually transmitted diseases. And sexual outercourse can give two people sexual satisfaction. It's important to know, however, that there are some risks involved. The greatest danger associated with sexual outercourse is that some consider it a "slippery slope" to sexual intercourse, meaning that some people may find it difficult to engage in certain behaviors—particularly mutual masturbation and petting—without taking the extra step and actually having intercourse. In addition, there is a possibility that even without actual intercourse taking place, semen can leak from the penis and enter the vagina during outercourse. Should this happen, pregnancy can occur.

The other thing to keep in mind about sexual outercourse is that even though it is not actually intercourse, it is still sexual intimacy. This means that it can carry the same emotional issues that apply to sexual intercourse. For that reason, it is a behavior that requires the same responsible thought—including decision making—as sexual intercourse.

Responsible Contraceptive Use

If you do decide to have sexual intercourse with someone, you need to understand the correct use of birth control. There are several different types of contraceptives, and each has its own advantages and disadvantages. To decide what kind is best for you, you might ask your doctor or clinician. There are also counselors at family planning centers whom you can talk to about this. (See the yellow pages of your phone book for local listings or check out one of the hotlines or national agencies listed in Chapter 7.) Or you might look at one of the books listed in the resource section, such as *Changing Bodies, Changing Selves* or *Straight Talk About Sexually Transmitted Diseases.*

One thing to keep in mind about using contraceptives is that they will not work at all unless you use them correctly *each and every time you have sex.* If, for example, you use a condom the right way one time but then the next time that you have sex, you don't have any condoms left and go ahead without any protection, you are not using contraceptives correctly. Each time you have sex without a condom, you are just as much at risk of becoming pregnant or causing a pregnancy as you would be if you had never used anything at all. Likewise, if a condom breaks, if the guy does not pull out properly, or if you have sex twice using the same condom, you might just as well not be using anything at all.

Another thing to remember about contraceptive use is that although all birth control provides some protection against pregnancy, not all contraceptives protect you from sexually transmitted diseases. The only form of birth control that offers some protection against *both* pregnancy and sexually transmitted diseases is the correct use of condoms and spermicidal foam with nonoxynol-9.

What follows is a list in alphabetical order of the most often used birth control devices currently available. The "barrier" methods, contraceptives that form a physical barrier that prevents the sperm from joining the egg, are listed first. You can buy some contraceptives at the supermarket or drug store; others require a doctor's prescription. Remember to consider the advantages and disadvantages of each option before making your decision.

Barrier Methods

Condoms

Condoms are sheaths made out of a type of plastic called latex. They fit snugly over the penis. When an orgasm, or climax, occurs, the condom catches and confines the semen that is ejaculated from the penis. This means that no semen enters the woman's vagina, which protects the woman from conception and pregnancy.

It may be a good idea to take a condom out of its package before you actually need to use one, just to see how it works. You can follow the instructions on the insert that comes inside a box of condoms or sometimes printed on the back of the individual package. In order to see the way that if fits over the penis, you can take a banana or cucumber and roll the condom over it. This too will give you some idea of the way it's supposed to cover the penis during sexual intercourse. Remember to leave some space at the tip for the semen.

When used correctly, condoms with spermicidal cream or foam offer protection against pregnancy 98 percent of the time. This means that if 100 couples were to use this method correctly and according to instructions, 2 of those couples would still become pregnant. For couples who use condoms but do not always do so correctly, the rate of effectiveness falls to 88 percent, which means that 12 out of 100 couples would become pregnant.

The main reason condoms do not offer complete protection against pregnancy is that they can sometimes leak or break, allowing semen to enter the vagina. For that reason, it's a good idea to use condoms with a spermicidal foam or cream. These additional contraceptives can be inserted in the vagina, and they can kill any sperm that leaks from the condom and enters the vagina.

In addition, condoms have to be used from the beginning all the way to the end of intercourse in order to be completely effective. A lot of couples end up using the condom only at the very end of intercourse, right before ejaculation, which can cause pregnancy (or disease) if semen leaks into the vagina before the condom is in place.

One possible disadvantage to using condoms is that since they need to be applied right before the beginning of sexual intercourse, putting them on can interfere with spontaneity and can be downright inconvenient.

On the other hand, a big advantage of condoms and foam is that they are extremely accessible and relatively inexpensive. Condoms cost anywhere from 25¢ to $2.50 each. Foam costs about $8 a container. When authorized by a doctor or at a clinic, condom costs are covered by Medicaid in some states. No doctor's prescription is required, and you can find both in virtually any drugstore or supermarket. In addition, they are the one form of birth control that involves the male as well as the female partner. For this reason, they may help some men to feel more involved and invested in the effort to prevent a pregnancy from occurring.

One final advantage to using condoms and foam is that they offer protection against not only pregnancy but sexually transmitted diseases (including AIDS). This is not to say that a couple who uses condoms and foam is completely protected from these diseases, but they do make infection less likely to occur.

Diaphragms

Like condoms and foam, the diaphragm is a method of birth control that provides a barrier between the sperm and the egg. A woman using the diaphragm can insert it up to six hours before she has sexual intercourse. Once inserted, the diaphragm covers the woman's cervix, which means it prevents most sperm from entering the uterus. Unfortunately, however, sperm can sometimes get around the diaphragm and into the woman's womb. This means that women who use diaphragms should also use a spermicidal cream or jelly, which they can apply to the diaphragm before it is inserted.

Diaphragms themselves are relatively inexpensive. They cost between $18 and $25, and this cost is covered by Medicaid. Also, they can be quite effective when used correctly. According to Planned Parenthood, diaphragms prevent pregnancy 94 percent of the time for women who use them with cream or jelly according to instructions. And diaphragms have almost no side effects, with the exception of urinary tract infections.

However, diaphragms also have several disadvantages. For one thing, when they are used without spermicidal cream or jelly, their effectiveness rate falls dramatically, to only 82 percent. In addition, although they are inexpensive, they are not available over the counter in drug stores but instead require a health care professional's prescription and also a proper fitting (vaginas vary in size, and the diaphragm must fit the woman's vagina correctly in order to be effective). This fitting, covered by Medicaid, costs between $50 and $100. Many women also find diaphragms inconvenient, because they do need to be inserted within six hours before intercourse, and, eventually, removed, washed, and put away. (Diaphragms should stay in the woman's vagina for at least eight hours after intercourse.) Also, if a couple wants to have intercourse more than once, they must insert more cream or jelly before each time.

Diaphragms can also cause urinary tract infections for some women. Finally, although the barrier formed by diaphragms and spermicidal cream and jelly can be an effective form of birth control, it does *not* provide any protection against sexually transmitted diseases, such as AIDS. For that reason, many women use both diaphragms plus cream or jelly *and* condoms, to protect as far as possible against both pregnancy and STDs.

Vaginal pouches

The newest barrier method of birth control is the vaginal pouch, also known as the "female condom." Like the diaphragm, the vaginal pouch is inserted into the vagina, and covers the cervix, blocking most sperm from entering the uterus. The pouch also covers the vulva. Easier to insert than the diaphragm, it can also be inserted right before sex. It should be thrown away right after intercourse has been completed. The vaginal pouch does not require a doctor's prescription. Another appealing aspect of the vaginal pouch is that when used with spermicidal foam, it can provide some protection against not only pregnancy but sexually transmitted diseases.

When used correctly, the vaginal pouch has a 94.8 percent effectiveness rate in preventing pregnancy. When used incorrectly, however, the effectiveness rate falls to 75.2 percent. Vaginal pouches costs about $2.50 apiece. When authorized by a private doctor or at a clinic, the cost is covered by Medicaid in some states.

Nonbarrier Methods

Birth control pills

Birth control pills are tablets that contain special hormones to prevent pregnancy based on a 28-day cycle that mimics a woman's natural menstrual cycle. Also known as oral contraceptives, they come in packets containing 21 or 28 pills. Women on birth control pills take one of these tablets each and every day if they use the 28-pill packet, or they take one pill each day for 21 days and then none for a week. Twenty-one of these pills actually contain hormones, and the other seven are "placebo," or fake, pills that are included so that the woman remains in the habit of taking the tablets each day.

The hormones in birth control pills keep a pregnancy from happening by preventing ovulation from occurring. Ovulation is a crucial part of the pregnancy process. Without it, there is no egg to be fertilized by the man's sperm. But even though an egg is not present to be fertilized, women taking birth control pills still dispel their uterus lining each month, which means that their menstrual periods still occur.

There are several advantages to taking birth control pills. First of all, they are convenient. There's no equipment to carry around, no need to put on a condom or insert a diaphragm at the last minute.

In addition, they are one of the most effective forms of contraception. When taken correctly and according to instructions, birth control pills are 99.1 to 99.5 percent effective. For women who don't take the pills properly— say, if they forget to take a tablet one day—the rate of effectiveness falls to 97 percent. Finally, some studies suggest that taking birth control pills can lessen a woman's chances of suffering ovarian cancer and cancer of the endometrius, or uterine lining.

Birth control pills have their disadvantages as well. To begin with, you can't just walk into a drug store and pick them up off the shelf. You need a prescription. So every woman interested in taking the pill must get her health care professional's go-ahead before she can do so. The cost for this examination ranges from about $35 to $125. Monthly packets of the pill cost between $15 and $25 apiece. The cost is usually less at a clinic and is covered by Medicaid.

In addition, birth control pills can cause health complications for some women. Some studies suggest, for example, that they may increase a woman's chances of suffering breast cancer. Women using oral contraceptives are also at a higher risk of experiencing harmful blood clots, particularly if they smoke. In fact, Planned Parenthood suggests that women who do choose to go on the pill quit smoking completely. Some women have experienced other unpleasant side effects, such as headaches, dizziness, mood swings, and weight gain.

Finally, although oral contraceptives are an effective form of birth control, they offer absolutely no protection whatsoever against sexually transmitted infections. For that reason, most health care professionals recommend birth control pills for women who are in monogamous relationships such as marriage.

Contraceptive foam and suppositories

Although health professionals strongly recommend that contraceptive foam and suppositories be used along with condoms, it is possible to use them on their own. Inserted into the vagina with a special device right before sexual intercourse, foam and suppositories prevent pregnancy by neutralizing, or killing, the sperm that enters the vagina before it can reach the woman's uterus.

Foam and suppositories are fairly inexpensive. Foam costs about $8 per container, and each container has 20 to 40 applications. Suppositories, usually sold in packages containing 20 applications, cost about $8 as well. When authorized by a doctor or at a clinic, the costs are covered by Medicaid in some states. They can be purchased over the counter at most drug stores. They are easy to insert, and unlike condoms or diaphragms, they do not need to be removed after intercourse. When used correctly and according to instructions, they are 94 percent effective in preventing pregnancy. Their success rate falls to 79 percent when used incorrectly.

When used in conjunction with a condom, foam and suppositories do provide some protection against sexually transmitted diseases. In addition, according to a 1996 study by the Food and Drug Administration, foams, jellies, and suppositories (and also condoms) that contain a chemical called nonoxynol provides some extra protection against chlamydia and gonorrhea, two sexually transmitted diseases.

Depo-Provera

Another recently approved form of birth control is Depo-Provera, the brand name for depotmedroxyprogesterone acetate (DMPA). Like Norplant, Depo-Provera is a hormonal type of contraception that is inserted once and lasts for a relatively long period of time. Rather than being inserted under the skin, however, Depo-Provera is given in the form of injections into the muscle of the woman's buttock or upper arm. These injections have to be repeated every 12 weeks in order for Depo-Provera to remain effective.

Like Norplant and birth control pills, Depo-Provera stops pregnancy from occurring by preventing ovulation. It is an effective form of birth control for 99.3 percent of all women who use it.

Depo-Provera has many of the same advantages as Norplant. Both require little day-to-day maintenance, although women using Depo-Provera do have to remember to receive additional injections every 12 weeks. Some studies reported by Planned Parenthood claim that Depo-Provera may have some health benefits for women who take them. It may, for example, decrease a woman's chances of suffering endometrial cancer (the endometrius is the lining of the uterus), and might also improve the condition of women with sickle-cell anemia or endometriosis (a condition that occurs when parts of the endometrium leak to other areas of the body).

Keep in mind that Depo-Provera is not a barrier method of birth control, which means that it does not lessen a couple's chances of transmitting infection. In addition, there is some evidence that may link Depo-Provera to an increased risk of breast cancer in the women who use it.

Like Norplant, Depo-Provera requires not only a prescription but a procedure. Some women find the idea of undergoing injections distasteful, although most Depo-Provera users experience only some mild discomfort during the injection process. The cost of the examination necessary for use of Depo-Provera ranges from $35 to $125. The cost of Depo-Provera itself is about $50. Each subsequent injection costs between $20 and $40. All costs are covered by Medicaid.

Emergency contraception (the morning-after pill)

There is one form of birth control that can act to prevent pregnancy *after* a couple has had sex. Called emergency contraception, or the morning-after pill, this type of protection is effective up to 72 hours after sexual intercourse. Since it has a powerful effect on a woman's system, it is usually used only when extreme measures are called for, and it is *not* recommended for regular use.

Emergency contraception consists of four pills, taken in two dosages. A woman will take the first two pills 24 to 72 hours after intercourse, and the second two pills 12 hours later. The pills contain the same hormones as oral contraceptives, Depo-Provera, and Norplant but in much higher dosages.

Morning-after pills do not have an extremely useful rate of effectiveness—they protect against pregnancy only 75 percent of the time they are used. In addition, they cause several side effects, including nausea, vomiting, and headaches.

Most significantly, however, if a woman taking these pills was already pregnant before the latest intercourse occurred, the pills will not abort the fetus but can damage it. For that reason, all women who take emergency contraception should have a pregnancy test before they take their first dosage of pills. A responsible clinic will administer such a test.

Norplant

Norplant, the brand name for levonorgestrel, is a relatively new form of contraception that many health care professionals recommend for young unmarried women. Like birth control pills, Norplant contains special hormones that work to prevent pregnancy. But rather than being swallowed, as oral contraceptives are, Norplant contains six capsules that are actually inserted under the skin of the woman—usually in the underside of her upper arm. The hormones are then released into the woman's system, where they act in much the same way as the chemicals in birth control pills do.

There are several advantages to this form of birth control. For one thing, it's long lasting. The hormones in the six inserted capsules provide protection against pregnancy for up to five years.

In a similar vein, it's an extremely low-maintenance form of contraception. A woman on birth control pills has to remember to take them every single day. But once Norplant is inserted, it can be forgotten about—again, for up to five years. This is an extremely important consideration, particularly for younger women, who often have trouble remembering to use birth control on a regular basis.

Finally, because Norplant is professionally inserted and removed, every woman who uses it does so correctly. The effectiveness rate for Norplant is therefore very high. According to Planned Parenthood, Norplant is an effective form of birth control for 99.66 percent of the women using it.

Perhaps Norplant's most significant disadvantage is that it does not provide protection against sexually transmitted diseases. This means that a woman with Norplant inserts would still have to use condoms and foam in order to lessen her chances of contracting AIDS or other SDTs. In addition, Norplant requires not only a prescription from a health-care professional but an actual medical procedure as well.

The cost of Norplant can also be a disadvantage for some women. According to Planned Parenthood, on average, Norplant insertion costs between $500 and $750, which includes the medical exam, the implants themselves, and the insertion by trained practitioners. This amounts to a little more than $100 a year over a five-year period. Removal of Norplant, which must be done after five years of use, generally costs an additional $50–$150.

When it first became available, Norplant insertion and removal was not covered by any major form of insurance; however, it is now covered in all 50 states by Medicaid. In addition, there is a Norplant foundation that provides free insertion and removal of the contraceptive to specially qualified low-income women. For more information about this, contact your local family planning center, or check one of the resources listed on pages 123–125 of this book.

Norplant does have some side effects, the most common of which are not serious. They include irregular bleeding between periods, no bleeding at all for months at a time, and longer-than-usual menstrual flow. Other, less common side effects of Norplant may include a possible scarring at insertion and removal site; weight gain or loss; nausea and dizziness; nervousness; sore breasts; and an increased chance of ectopic (outside the uterus) pregnancy in the unlikely event that a pregnancy occurs.

The rhythm method (periodic abstinence)

You learned in the last chapter that the only form of birth control that provides 100 percent protection against pregnancy and sexually transmitted diseases is abstinence. When practiced periodically, abstinence is not nearly as effective, although it does have several advantages.

Couples who practice periodic abstinence (also known as the "rhythm method") refrain from sexual intercourse during the time of the month when the woman is ovulating. It's not always easy to know when ovulation occurs. Some women track their cycles by taking their temperature each day of the month. They find that their temperature is slightly higher during the days they are ovulating.

Temperature can be taken in one of several ways. Most people do so by putting a digital thermometer (available over the counter at drug stores) underneath the tongue until a beep sounds. Some people take their temperature anally, others under the arm. There are also thermometers that take temperature readings through the outer ear. This method takes less time, but the thermometers themselves are significantly more expensive than the basic digital ones.

It's important to use the same method of taking temperature each time it is done. Readings do vary according to the method used. Anal temperature, for example, is usually about one degree higher than oral temperature, and about two degrees higher than temperatures taken under the arm. Ear temperatures are usually around the same as oral temperatures.

Taking temperatures in order to determine the time of ovulation is not always reliable. Although ovulation is one factor that can affect a person's temperature, there are many other ones as well. Minor viral infections, for example, can cause a slight increase in one's temperature, as can taking a bath or shower, or drinking a cold or hot beverage, right before temperature is taken.

There are also ovulation kits available over the counter that can determine ovulation by testing the chemical balance of the woman's urine every day of the month. These kits are fairly expensive—they usually cost about $35 each.

The investment in a thermometer or a monthly ovulation kit is the only expense required for a couple practicing periodic abstinence. Another advantage of this method is that it has no side effects.

There are, however, several disadvantages. The most obvious of these is that it takes a great deal of work to practice periodic abstinence successfully. A woman who tracks her cycle by taking her temperature, for example, should do it every day before she even gets out of bed, preferably at the same time each morning, in order to get the most accurate reading. Even the most devoted couples are likely forget to follow this procedure every once in a while, or to make a mistake in how they read or record a temperature. Teens' menstrual cycles tend to be more irregular than adults', which can make tracking it frustrating, complicated, and less accurate.

In addition, there is a large discrepancy in the success rate between couples who practice periodic abstinence according to instructions and those who don't. According to Planned Parenthood, this method of birth control can be 99 percent effective when practiced correctly, but only 80 percent or so when it's not. In addition, it can be very hard to choose not to have sex, especially if you are used to a sexual relationship, just because of what the thermometer said that morning.

Finally, it's important to remember that when a couple who practice periodic abstinence do have sex, they usually do so without another form of contraception. This means that when used alone, this method of birth control can most certainly not be relied upon to provide protection against sexually transmitted diseases.

Choosing Wisely

Tonya did finally decide that she was ready to have sexual intercourse with Jack. It was a big deal to both of them. They both decided that they would be as responsible as they could be regarding birth control. They started by using condoms and foam, and then Tonya went to a family planning clinic and got a prescription for birth control pills. Tonya and Jack were wise, and lucky too. The sexual part of their relationship didn't remove any of the emotional intimacy they had formed, and the fact that they were so close and loved one another before they actually slept together seemed to make the sexual part of the relationship more pleasurable for both. And because they were using contraceptives correctly and responsibly, they knew that they were keeping Tonya's chances of getting pregnant about as low as possible for two sexually active people.

Contraceptives do provide a variety of options for couples involved in a responsible relationship and who have decided to become sexually active. In fact, an important part of being in a mature sexual relationship is knowing how to use birth control methods in the appropriate manner. It's important to remember that the proper use of contraceptives is the responsibility of both partners. It should never be left to just one partner or the other to be sure the method chosen is being used correctly. If, for example, a couple has chosen to use birth control pills, it is the responsibility not only of the woman but of her partner as well to make sure she remembers to take them every day. Jack, in fact, asks Tonya all the time if she's remembered to take her pill. Sometimes it drives Tonya crazy, but in truth she appreciates the fact that Jack cares enough to be involved. In addition, both partners need to figure out how to protect themselves and each other against sexually transmitted diseases.

Finally, remember that contraceptives are not perfect forms of birth control. Even when used correctly, unintended pregnancies can and do occur. The next chapter examines the options available to those teenagers who do become pregnant.

4

Options for
Pregnant Teens

Tess can't believe it. Sam is the first guy she's been interested in since Rob. She has so little time to be with him—usually he comes over after Stephanie and Tess's mother have gone to bed. The good news is that she really cares about him, and she thinks he feels the same way about her. The really bad news, though, is that even though they've used condoms every time they had sex, she has gotten pregnant again anyway, probably because they'd used them without foam.

Now Tess doesn't know what to do. She knows she can't keep this child: She can barely afford Stephanie, so how could she manage another? On the other hand, what are her choices? Abortion? Adoption? Tess needs some advice, and she needs it fast.

Deep down, Trey wasn't surprised when Valerie told him. Of course she's pregnant. That's what happens when you don't use birth control. When Trey first found out, he was pretty angry with Valerie. Why didn't she use anything? But he knew that it was his responsibility, too. And he had blown it.

What's really weird for Trey is how excited Valerie is about it. And she is. It's kind of cool to be pregnant, she thinks to herself. I'll get a lot of gifts like everyone else in school who's had a baby did. And anyway, a baby will love me. How hard can it be?

Trey wouldn't mind talking to Valerie about options. Do they have to keep the baby? And what about abortion? But Valerie wants to have and keep their child. He knows what his parents will say, and he's not looking forward to telling them.

Robin, on the other hand, was shocked and horrified. Matt had told her he knew what he was doing. "Don't worry too much about birth control," he'd said, "we'll use condoms when you're right in between periods, but the rest of the time we don't need them." She had believed him, and now, she's just found out that she's pregnant.

The first thing I'm going to do, she thought, is find out how to get an abortion. Then I'm going to kill Matt for doing this to me. But when Matt called her later that day, Robin couldn't stay mad at him. She couldn't even tell him what was going on with her. I'll wait until I see him, she thought. We need to discuss this face-to-face.

Teenagers who become pregnant have three choices: They can have an abortion; they can put the child up for adoption; or they can have and raise the baby themselves. None of these choices are easy ones. Each one has its own set of consequences. If you are a pregnant teen reading this chapter to gain information about the options available to you, remember that ultimately this decision must feel right to *you* since whichever choice you finally make will affect you and the fetus you are carrying more than anyone else.

Keep in mind that no matter how much you read about these options, it may help you just as much to talk to an adult you trust—a member of your family, a teacher, a coach, or a religious or community leader. You might also be more comfortable talking with someone you've never met before but who knows enough about pregnancy to offer advice without judgment. You may want to make an appointment at a local family planning center, such as Planned Parenthood. You can usually find numbers for these places in your local phone book, or check the last chapter of this book for possible resources.

Option 1: Abortion

Abortion is the removal of the fetus from the woman's uterus. The procedure should be done by a trained professional, in general during the first 20 weeks of pregnancy. According to a 1996 study by Planned Parenthood, about 35 percent of all teen pregnancies end in abortion.

Of all the choices available to pregnant teens, abortion is by far the most discussed, the most argued about, and the most controversial. It's also the most mercurial—laws, rules, and regulations; its legal status; the definitions surrounding it; and the rights of women to choose it change constantly. This section will offer you the latest information concerning your own rights to have an abortion, as well as the advantages, disadvantages, and potential consequences of that choice.

A Stormy History

Until 1973, abortion was illegal in most U.S. states. This does not mean that the procedure was never performed, however. Many women who were pregnant would seek what were called "back street" abortionists. These people were not always medically trained and sometimes used unsanitary equipment when conducting the procedure. As a result, the women who got illegal abortions—a relatively safe and simple procedure under normal circumstances —were often injured, some so seriously that they were never able to have children again. Some women died.

In 1973, a case by the name of *Roe v. Wade* came before the U.S. Supreme Court. The plaintiff, a woman who used the alias Jane Roe to protect her privacy, had wanted to have a lawful and safe abortion—one by a trained medical doctor in a legal facility—and had not been able to under Texas law. The defendants in the case—originally Henry B. Wade, Texas district attorney—argued that abortion is not a medical procedure but a crime against an innocent life. In short, they believed that abortion was murder and therefore illegal.

The arguments for both sides in *Roe v. Wade* were deeply felt. And the seven Supreme Court justices who voted on the case were split on their opinions. Four of them believed "Jane Roe" and all other women in the United States had the right to have abortions during the first part of their pregnancies. Three of them disagreed, stating that government had the right to outlaw abortion, which they considered a crime against another person. However, there was a majority, and *Roe v. Wade* led to the passage of a law that made abortion a legal procedure.

Pro-Life vs. Pro-Choice

The *Roe v. Wade* decision made it illegal for states to limit the rights of women to get abortions during early pregnancy —the first three months, when the fetus is least developed and the procedure is safest for the mother. But that one court case has not ended the controversy surrounding abortion. Throughout the United States, there are groups that call themselves "pro-life." In their view, the unborn fetus is a live, unborn person with rights of its own.

Pro-life activists gather each year in Washington, D.C., on the anniversary of the *Roe v. Wade* case to protest the decision. They also hold marches and protests in other places, including outside some family planning centers such as Planned Parenthood. Often, their goal is to talk to pregnant women who may be thinking about getting an abortion, to convince them to reconsider. The vast majority of pro-life gatherings are peaceful ones. However, over the years, some pro-life activists have committed crimes against doctors who perform abortions and have bombed or vandalized clinics where abortions are performed or, in same cases, discussed. Sometimes, too, antiabortion activists are so eager to convince women entering clinics not to have abortions that their efforts amount to harassment: yelling at the women, showing them graphic pictures of abortion, and in some cases physically blocking their way.

People on the "pro-choice" side of the issue believe by contrast that the issue of abortion is a private one that each woman should be allowed to make for herself during the first part of her pregnancy. Some people argue that those who believe in woman's right to choose actually see abortion as a form of birth control, rather than as an option if birth control has failed. Certainly no official pro-choice organization holds this view. Rather, most pro-choicers say that a woman has the right to make this very difficult decision for herself during the first part of her pregnancy. They do not believe that the government should be allowed to interfere with this decision by limiting this right.

Then there are those who do not exactly consider abortion murder, as many pro-life groups do, but who also believe that generally, women should not have that right except under certain circumstances. They do not support a woman's right to choose, but they do believe that abortion might be appropriate in certain situations: when the woman's life is in danger because of the pregnancy, when the fetus has been found to have a major deformity, or when the woman became pregnant as a result of rape or incest. No one really agrees about what these circumstances should be, however, and there are many arguments among this group.

The Question of Viability

One of the most political aspects of the entire abortion debate is whether a woman should be able to choose to abort a fetus at any time during her pregnancy. According to *Roe v. Wade,* legal abortions can occur only before the developing fetus achieves "viability." In simpler terms, this means that as soon as the fetus reaches the stage in development at which it could survive outside of the mother's womb, with or without medical help, that woman loses the right to abort.

Most studies find the minimum time for achieving viability is 23 to 24 weeks from the date of the pregnant woman's last menstrual period. This means that under *Roe v. Wade,* most abortions in the first five months of pregnancy are legal. And in fact, most abortions are performed before the fetus is 20 weeks old.

In the past, some doctors did perform abortions after 20 weeks in a woman's pregnancy. Federal legislators tried in both 1996 and 1997 to outlaw these procedures, called "partial-birth" abortions, but their efforts fell short both years when President Clinton vetoed their bills. Even so, the vast majority of partial birth abortions that occur today are those that are performed in extreme circumstances—usually when the mother's life is at stake.

Take a moment to consider the sides of the abortion argument. Do you think a woman should have the right to choose whether to have this procedure? Or do you think all abortions are murder, and that no one should be allowed to harm an unborn fetus? If you are in favor of choice, do you think there's a time in pregnancy when a woman should no longer be allowed to decide to have an abortion?

Parental Involvement

Federal legislation concerning abortion has been modified in several ways since the original *Roe v. Wade* decision.

One of those changes has allowed states to require women under the age of 21 to notify their parents before undergoing the procedure. As of this writing, 28 states have chosen to make this requirement. Some states call not only for parental notification but for parental permission as well. In some cases, as in Minnesota, both parents must give their permission for an abortion to be performed, even if the teenager is not living with both parents or has not seen one parent in several years.

Some groups have cheered this decision because it involves the family in what can be a very traumatic decision. Others argue that such requirements are detrimental to a person's right to choose abortion, preventing some teenagers from opting for the procedure out of fear at what their parents might do. This is especially true, this argument continues, for those in families where teens may have suffered abuse at the hands of their parents. Some teenagers, in fact, become pregnant as a result of being sexually molested by a father or male guardian. Why, advocates ask, should a teenager have to rely on permission from such a parent to obtain an abortion?

According to the American Civil Liberties Union, 61 percent of teenagers who obtain an abortion in states that do *not* require parental notification *do* inform their parents before undergoing the procedure. This suggests that most teenagers do want to involve their parents in this important decision—though clearly, many do not.

What are your thoughts on this subject? Do you think a teenager should be able to get an abortion without informing her parents? Or do you think families should be informed before this procedure can be performed?

Insurance

Another limit was placed on *Roe v. Wade* in 1976. That year Congress passed the Hyde Amendment, which excluded abortion from the list of comprehensive health services paid for by the federal Medicaid program. While both standard insurance programs and Health Maintenance Organization (HMO) packages will pay for a covered woman's abortion, women in most states who are on the Medicaid plan do not have coverage for this procedure. (Sixteen states do currently provide Medicaid funding for abortions.) This means that most of the nation's poorest people—with the exception of those who became pregnant as the result of rape or incest—have to pay for abortions themselves.

Again, this issue has its proponents and opponents. Those who agree with the Hyde Amendment stress that an act that they consider to be murder should not be offered to women as part of an insurance package. They add that perhaps the expense of the abortion (which usually costs about $200 to $400) will discourage people not only from seeking the procedure but from getting pregnant in the first place.

Those who believe that insurance should cover abortions for poor people have a different view. They stress that withholding insurance from people will not actually discourage pregnancy. Most people who become pregnant, including teenagers, do so by accident. What withholding insurance *does* do, this argument continues, is to make it difficult and sometimes impossible for poor women to obtain abortions.

Emotional Issues

Robin, Tess, and Valerie all need to make decisions about their pregnancies. Neither Tess nor Valerie can bring herself to think about having an abortion. For Tess, a practicing Catholic, it's a religious issue. She knows she hasn't been such a strict Catholic all her life, having premarital sex and even giving birth out of wedlock. Still, abortion is where she draws the line.

Valerie's objection to abortion has less to do with her religious beliefs than with her own instincts. The moment she found out she was pregnant, she knew she couldn't harm what was inside her—it already felt alive, and a part of her and Trey.

Robin, on the other hand, isn't so sure how she feels about abortion. She does know, though, that she doesn't feel able to bring a child into the world at this stage of her life, for several reasons. First of all, she's through with Matt. He's been a jerk about the whole pregnancy thing, and she doesn't want to have anything to do with him. That means it will be up to Robin alone to bring up her baby.

Her family is another issue. Robin doesn't feel that she can tell her parents about being pregnant. She thinks they would be unable to deal not only with her condition but with the additional fact that she's no longer a virgin. Her father might even hit her—he's done it before when he's caught Robin coming home in the middle of the night. How could they ever help her raise a baby? Robin can't bear the thought of her father hitting her child, but she knows that it's a risk if she stays at home. She also knows that she can't move out and live on her own at this point. She can't afford it, for one thing, and for another, she's not sure how she would manage going to school and being a single parent at the same time.

School, in fact, is a third concern for Robin. She had always assumed she would finish high school, go to college, and then get a job and figure out the rest of her life. It's a sequence of events she's felt comfortable with, and even excited about at times. She feels a little selfish about this, but she doesn't want to give it up.

For all these reasons, Robin is considering having an abortion. But she has concerns, doubts, and fears about the procedure as well. For one thing, she worries about how safe it is. Will she be able to have children later on, when she's ready to, or will an abortion do harm to her reproductive system? And how does she feel about what she's doing to her unborn fetus? Is it a child yet? Is it murder?

Robin ends up calling her neighborhood Planned Parenthood, and she sets up a meeting with a social worker there named Helen. The first thing Helen tells Robin is that abortion is a safe procedure that will not have any negative effect on her ability to conceive at a later time. But she also says that Robin's concerns about the procedure are common ones and that she will simply have to make up her own mind about them. Abortion, the social worker adds, is not a procedure like going to the dentist—something you do one day and can forget about the next. What you're doing, she says, is something that will stay with you in one way or another for the rest of your life.

On the other hand, Helen tells Robin, don't be too hard on yourself for being selfish. In the long run, it could be that having the abortion is much *less* selfish than bringing into the world a child to whom you can't give your best at this point in your life.

After a sleepless night and a difficult day at school—she just couldn't concentrate on anything—Robin makes the decision to have an abortion. Two weeks later, she has the procedure. The pregnancy is over, and Robin knows that for her, it was the right thing to do. Even so, she realizes that Helen is right. It's something she'll never forget.

Adoption

Tess knows how difficult it's been to be the parent of just *one* child. Raising another, she thinks, is something she's neither financially nor emotionally capable of doing right now. That kind of situation, she reasons, would be unfair not only to herself but to Stephanie, and ultimately, to the new baby as well. Because of Tess's religious beliefs, abortion simply isn't a possible choice for her. But she is considering adoption.

If Tess chooses this option, she will carry her pregnancy to term, have the baby, and then give the child up for another family to raise. There are many merits to adoption, and of course some disadvantages as well. Tess feels relieved, for example, that she will not have to undergo an abortion, that she will not have to raise a child that she doesn't really want, that the child *will* be raised by parents who do want him or her and who will provide the support and attention that she herself isn't capable of giving right now.

On the other hand, Tess knows what it's like to be pregnant, to feel life inside her, to go through labor and birth, and finally to see the baby you've created and nurtured inside you for nine months. She doesn't know how she can possibly go through all that with the knowledge that the child she is bearing will not be hers to raise.

Nevertheless, Tess is determined to do what's best for her unborn child. The next day she finds some free time, goes to the library, and does some research on how to place her child for adoption.

Two Possible Processes

In general, there are two types of adoption processes available in the United States. The first of these, agency adoptions, are done through accredited organizations. These agencies put those interested in adopting a child through rigorous screening processes known as "home study." It can take several months for all the paperwork to be approved for these potential parents, but in the end it's an excellent way of ensuring that any child who is adopted —whether born in the United States or in a foreign country —will end up in a loving home.

Agencies handle roughly 50 percent of all adoptions in the United States. The others are done in a more private manner and are known as "independent adoptions." Children who are adopted in this fashion are placed directly with their new families by the biological parents or guardians. Usually a lawyer is present to advise both sets of parents of their rights, and to make other legal arrangements.

Many biological parents prefer independent adoptions to agency ones because they want to have direct control over who the new parents of their child will be. They may also want to have the option of having some sort of relationship with the child. On the other hand, some people may find independent adoption more emotionally difficult than agency adoptions. Not every person about to have a child knows trustworthy people who want to adopt a child. Also, there are those who have mixed feelings about staying in touch with their child after the adoption has occurred. It's up to the biological parents to decide which process they are more comfortable with.

Legal Issues

Forty-five states in the United States allow a minor to place a child in an adopting home without obtaining parental consent. There are four states that do require parental consent for minors. They are Alabama, New Hampshire (if the mother is unwed), Oklahoma (if the mother is under 16), and West Virginia. A fifth, Indiana, allows a parent under 18 to place a child in an adopting home without parental consent unless the court decides it is in the best interest of the child to have that consent.

Another legal issue concerning adoption has to do with biological parents' rights to reclaim their child after the adoption has already occurred. There have been several well-publicized cases in which biological parents (of all ages) have changed their minds after an adoption has been completed and decided that they'd like to keep their child after all. Most states ensure that a biological parent does have the right to reclaim his or her child, usually within the first six months of the child's life.

In addition, many states now grant adopted children the right to find out who their biological parents are. Such states keep open records of each adoption performed there. As laws have changed over the years, some states that formerly had closed records, so that neither birth parents nor children could find each other, have since opened their records. These are issues you should be aware of if you are considering putting your baby up for adoption.

Emotional Concerns

Tess finds it comforting to know that she is making what seems to her a responsible and unselfish choice. She feels that she has put the needs of both children—Stephanie and her unborn baby—in front of her own. She thinks that providing both of them with a loving home—even if they're separate ones—is the most important consideration throughout her pregnancy.

Those kinds of thoughts have made the nine months of pregnancy more bearable for Tess. There have been times that she has had second thoughts and serious doubts about her decision. Explaining it to Stephanie has been wrenching, and half of her friends think that she should keep the baby.

Tess's thoughts on adoption are not at all uncommon for women in her situation. Like abortion, adoption does have its emotional issues. Some people may find it rewarding to know that the child they are carrying will make some loving parents very happy. Others, however, may feel angry, sad, despairing, or guilty that they have to go through the difficulties of pregnancy and the pain of labor only to give the child up to someone else. And, of course, many people dread the loss, which marks not only abortion but adoption as well. Adoption can be viewed as an act of giving, or as an instance of profound loss. Many biological parents, in fact, view it as both. Like having an abortion, placing a child in an adoptive home is a decision that stays with a person her entire life.

There are other issues surrounding adoption that make this option complex. For example, according to the National Information Clearinghouse, it is easier in the United States to find adoptive parents for white children than for children of color. This may be one reason that a 1996

Planned Parenthood study indicates that most teenagers who do choose adoption are white and from middle-class backgrounds. Another reason is that people of color are far more likely to raise the child themselves or in some part of the extended family. All in all, according to Planned Parenthood, about 10 percent of teenagers who carry their children to term choose to place them in adopted homes.

A Child of Your Own

Valerie and Trey have both broken the news to their respective parents. Valerie's mother was furious at first, but then she told Valerie that she can't turn her back on her daughter and her daughter's baby. Trey's parents did just what he thought they would: They want him to stay with Valerie. "The three of you can move in here with us," they said. "There's room for all of you." Trey's still not sure how he feels. Everything's happening so fast. He feels left out of a lot of the decision making. Shouldn't he and Valerie talk more about what all this is going to mean? Shouldn't it be up to him to decide who he's going to live with and when that will be? For a while he thought about running away. But in the end he decided not to.

Valerie, in the meantime, is excited about telling her friends that she's pregnant—maybe they'll throw her a shower—and about having something to think about other than school. Her mother, though, is far more skeptical. "You have no idea what you're in for, Val. Wait until the baby is born. Then you'll see what I mean."

According to the government study *Monthly Vital Statistics Report* (December 1996), about 500,000 babies are born each year to teen parents. About 90 percent of teenagers who carry their babies to term choose to raise their children themselves.

Your Rights

Every new parent has legal rights and responsibilities. If you are pregnant and thinking about becoming a parent, it's important for you to know what you are entitled to, as well as what you are responsible for. This chapter provides you with this basic information. For more on the experience of being a parent, see Chapter 5.

As you learned in Chapter 1, if you are a teenage girl and you elect to bring your child up yourself, as of 1998, you can qualify for welfare assistance if you remain at home with your parents or legal guardian until you reach the age of 21 and show that you are preparing for future employment by remaining in school.

In addition to these requirements, a teen parent—or both teen parents, if they are living together—needs to be financially eligible to receive welfare, earning less than a certain amount of money per year in order to qualify for welfare coverage. The actual requirements vary from state to state, as do the amount of the monthly payments themselves.

Welfare provides qualifying families not only with a monthly paycheck but with health care coverage through Medicaid and some housing options as well. To find out more about what you are entitled to, check your local phone book for your state or local welfare department, or see if you can find a local welfare rights group.

If you are a teenage mother and you want to share responsibility for your child with his or her father, you do have the right to do so. In most states, there are legal actions teenage mothers can take to name the fathers of their children, or establish the paternity, without the father's permission. The new welfare law has streamlined this process, making it easier than ever to establish legal paternity. Once the child's paternity has been established, the father is then legally responsible—under threat of arrest on the grounds of negligence—to help support the child financially.

Your Responsibilities

Parents have the legal responsibility to take care of their children financially until they become legal adults at age 18. This means seeing that children are properly fed, clothed, and housed. Parents are responsible for their children's education and for the care that children receive during the day if the parents are at school, work, or elsewhere.

If you are a parent, you also have moral responsibilities toward your child. It is your job to protect him or her from emotional or physical abuse and to provide him or her with a safe and supportive atmosphere at all times.

Keep in mind that fathers are just as responsible for the care of their children as mothers are. The new welfare laws require that a father who is not living with his child nevertheless share financial responsibility with the mother. Fathers who fail to provide this child support can be denied welfare payments. Fathers who are not on welfare who fail to share financial responsibilities can be prosecuted to the full extent of the law.

A Life-Changing Decision

The decision to keep a child while you are still a teenager is, once again, a very important one. Should you decide to do it, you have sacrificed a major portion of your life for another person who is completely dependent on you. You will be less likely to finish high school, attend college, and make a decent living than your peers who do not have a child.

That said, there are some rewards to being a parent that cannot be denied. You get to watch your child grow into a well-rounded individual. You have the pleasure—as well as the pain—of creating your own family. And you have the chance to give your child the love and support that you yourself had—or wanted—as a child.

Here are some statements from teenagers who have decided to raise their children on their own, taken from Inn Sight Teen Parents website (http://www.chatlink.com/~nbetween/nsighttp.htm, at the time the information was found; the site no longer exists). They discuss both the joys and the hardships of teen parenting.

Jessica, age 20: "The best rewards about being a parent and a teenager at the same time are: seeing my child play, learn, and grow. I am still learning about life while my child is also learning. I love seeing my child be happy and content. . . . I, as a parent [,] am also learning, because I am still young. I am learning to have patience with my son. I always don't know what to do when something is wrong with my son. There could be the simplest thing wrong with him and I will panic. For example, he will cry and cry and there wouldn't be anything I could do to quiet him down. . . ."

Frances, age 20: "The difficulties of being a parent and a teenager at the same time are numerous. You have to deal with issues such as trying to finish high school and be a responsible mother. Other issues are financial and emotional. Trying to finish school without kids can be a task, but when you have two small children you reach a whole new level of stress. No matter how bad you want to press snooze on the alarm clock you know there are lunches to be made, bathes [sic] to be given . . . Then you have to get yourself ready on time. . . . Homework is another problem when you have kids. There never seems to be time to sit down and study. Therefore you need to stay up after they're in bed just to do homework, resulting in the desire to press the snooze button each morning. . . ."

Shawn, age 19: "The difficulties of being a parent and a teenager at the same time are having to go to school while also having to pay the bills. . . . It's hard getting up in the middle of the night and then having to go to school in the morning. Then when you get out of school you have to go home and get ready for work.

"A lot of teen parents don't have high school diplomas let alone a college degree. You have to take a low-paying job just to stay ahead.

"People are rude to teen parents. A lot of people give you dirty looks. You don't get the same respect as an older parent.

"In conclusion, I think being a teen parent is very difficult, but I do love both of my daughters very much."

5

What It Means to Be a Teen Parent

Tess adored Stephanie from the first time she laid eyes on her—and it took every bit of that love to get them both through Stephanie's first year of life. First, there was the agony of the labor itself. Rob wasn't there to hold her hand, although her mother was with her. For 20 hours Tess screamed in pain.

When Stephanie was born, Tess spent one night at the hospital with her baby. Then they were both released and sent home. Every two hours Stephanie was hungry. She let Tess know this by crying loudly until she was fed. And every time Tess nursed Stephanie, she had to change her diaper as well. This process went on 24 hours a day—there was no relief at night.

Besides, sometimes Stephanie cried when she wasn't hungry. Sometimes, in fact, it seemed that Stephanie cried for no reason at all. At those times, there was nothing Tess could do to calm her down. This happened every night, for three hours at a time, until Stephanie was six months old.

There were times that Tess wanted to lock Stephanie in a closet or leave her outside—anything to get some peace and quiet for a change. Looking back on it now, Tess can't believe they both survived. She knows it's something she never wants to do on her own again.

The doctors told Valerie that her son was a low birth-weight baby. When he was born, Sean weighed only 4 pounds 3 ounces. He was so tiny that the doctors weren't sure he'd make it. Sean spent the first few weeks of his life in the intensive care unit of the hospital. Valerie stayed in the hospital too. Trey visited both of them there, and held Valerie's hand while she nursed Sean. Finally, the doctors said Sean was ready to go home.

Now Valerie and Sean are both living at Trey's mother's home. Valerie wakes up every morning at 5:00 to feed and dress the baby. Then Trey's mother cares for him until noon, when Valerie, who's on a reduced schedule at school, comes home for the day.

Valerie and Trey are beginning to argue about money. He thinks she needs to get a job, but she doesn't know how she'll handle work and school and Sean at the same time. She's tired all the time from her late nights and the early mornings—how could she possibly manage a job as well?

Sleepless nights, seemingly endless crying spells, a non-stop flow of dirty diapers . . . for new parents of every age, the reality of having a child can be stunning. If you are pregnant now—or about to become a teen father—you may already have heard all about what awaits you. And you may be wondering whether it really is as bad as all that. After all, people have been raising children for as long as there's been human life on earth. How hard can it be?

The answer is not a simple one, but you should know first and foremost that no one finds it easy to be a parent. Some people are more prepared for it than others, which can make it less surprising. And, of course, some babies arc easier than others. But on the whole, if you are expecting a child, it's important to understand that just about everything you hear about the hardships of raising a child is true. This chapter can give you some guidelines as to what to expect, but the reality of your new responsibility may very well not hit you until your baby is born.

Prenatal Care

One of the most important things you can do for your new baby (let's say it's a girl) is to begin taking care of her before she is born. This means eating healthful, nutritious foods; taking vitamins in their recommended dosages; avoiding such unhealthful substances as alcohol, cigarettes and perhaps caffeine, and seeing a health care professional on a regular basis. It can be hard to follow this regimen, and not every teenager does so. In fact, according to Planned Parenthood statistics from 1996, nearly 30 percent of teenage parents give their children less than adequate prenatal care.

Most doctors recommend that women who are pregnant come in for checkups every four weeks until the last two months of their term, when the visits increase to once every two weeks, and then once every week. At the first visit, the doctor will give you a full pelvic exam, including a pap smear, which is a special test the doctor does to check your cervix for any diseases or infections. You will also receive a blood test at this first visit, to determine whether you might need to take nutritional supplements in addition to the prenatal vitamins that every pregnant woman should take every day. The blood test can also detect the presence of some infections such as German measles or toxoplasmosis (an infection that can be carried by household cats and that can harm or damage a fetus if contracted by the mother while pregnant) that may pose a health threat to your unborn child. Most doctors offer an AIDS test as well, although you are not required to take it.

Until your final trimester, most of your prenatal visits after the first one will be less involved. Your weight, blood pressure, and urine will be tested. Your doctor will listen to your baby's heartbeat and feel your uterus to make sure the fetus is alive and growing. During these visits, you should feel free to ask as many questions as possible. The doctor is there not only to check on the health of your baby but to help you through your pregnancy as well. You may also want to invest in a prenatal birth book (or borrow one from your local library), such as *What to Expect When You're Expecting* by Arlene Eisenberg, Heidi E. Murkoff, and Sandee E. Hathaway. During your final month of pregnancy, the doctor will begin checking the position of your baby—whether she is head down in the traditional position, or breech, which means that the baby's buttocks will appear first if the baby is born vaginally. As your due date approaches, your doctor will also examine how much your cervix has dilated (expanded). This is an important indication of how close you are to going into labor.

Medications, Cigarettes, and Alcohol

It's especially important that you check with your doctor before taking any medications or other substances that might interfere with the health of your baby, even aspirin, cough medicine, or other over-the-counter products. If you must take something and cannot call your doctor, at least check the labels of medications such as ibuprofen, acetaminophen, aspirin, and other preparations. The labels often let you know if the substance you are taking is safe during pregnancy.

Remember that alcohol, tobacco, and other drugs, including marijuana, are all off limits entirely until after your baby is born. Valerie, who has a heavy cigarette habit, had a great deal of trouble quitting smoking during pregnancy. She ended up cutting down from two packs a day to one, but it is quite possible that Sean's low birth weight was caused by the cigarettes she did smoke while she was pregnant with him.

It may seem strange that the cigarettes Valerie smoked could have affected the growth of her unborn child. If the cigarettes didn't do any visible damage to Valerie, you may think, how could they have that kind of effect on Sean? The answer is that everything a mother puts into her body —whether through eating, drinking, or smoking—crosses the placenta and reaches her unborn child. The chemicals in cigarettes are no exception to this rule. One of these substances, carbon monoxide, cuts down the amount of oxygen that reaches the fetus. Another chemical, nicotine, limits the amount of both oxygen and nutrients that reach the fetus.

The children of women who smoke when they are pregnant are at an increased risk of being born at a lower-than-normal birth weight, which is what happened to Sean. Because of his weight, Sean is more vulnerable to infections such as anemia and jaundice, and may also suffer delays in physical and emotional development. Low birth-weight babies are also at higher risk of suffering mental retardation.

Studies show that women who smoke when they are pregnant are also at higher risk of stillbirth (when the baby is born dead), ectopic pregnancy (when the fetus embeds itself and develops in the fallopian tube rather than the uterus, a very dangerous and sometimes fatal situation for both mother and child), and premature birth (when the baby is born before it is full term, which is 37 weeks in the uterus). Once it is born, babies of smoking mothers are at twice the risk of sudden infant death syndrome (death due to unknown causes of an otherwise healthy baby during the first year of life) as are the babies of women who don't smoke.

Alcohol is another drug to be avoided during pregnancy. The major risk associated with alcohol is a complication called fetal alcohol syndrome, or FAS. Babies with FAS are lighter and shorter than normal babies and never develop as fully as healthy children. FAS children usually have small heads and sometimes have abnormal facial features. They have poor or no control of their muscles and often suffer severe heart defects. In addition, FAS babies usually have extreme behavioral difficulties. They are often hyperactive, are acutely nervous, and have extremely short attention spans. Finally, most of them are mentally retarded. In fact, according to *Planning for Pregnancy, Birth, and Beyond*, a book published in 1995 by the American College of Obstetricians and Gynecologists, FAS is the most common cause of mental retardation in babies.

Other Drugs

Like cigarettes and alcohol, all drugs can cross the placenta and damage the growing fetus. Marijuana, for example, contains carbon monoxide (also found in cigarettes), which as you know by now can cut down the amount of oxygen that reaches the fetus and slow down development.

Cocaine also contains harmful chemicals and is one of the most dangerous substances a woman can take while she is pregnant. Babies born to mothers who abuse cocaine tend to grow more slowly and have smaller heads and are more vulnerable to brain injury than are babies born to mothers who don't abuse drugs. In addition, cocaine can cause a serious complication during pregnancy called "abrupto placentae," which occurs when the uterus becomes detached from the placenta. Abrupto placentae can cause bleeding and premature labor, and it can be fatal to the unborn child.

In addition, pregnant women who use cocaine are at increased risk of high blood pressure, heart attacks, or strokes. Moreover, cocaine is an addictive drug, which means that people who take it become physically dependent on it. Thus the babies of women who are addicted to cocaine can be born with the same addiction. This means that these babies begin life with a severe drug dependency and must go through intense drug withdrawal if they have any hope of surviving.

Another physically addictive drug is heroin. Its effects on the unborn child are as serious as those of cocaine. Studies show that the children of women who use heroin while pregnant are more likely to be born prematurely, to suffer low birth weight, and to have behavioral problems than are the babies of nonusers. As with cocaine, heroin addiction is a condition that can be passed from mother to child. Heroin is such a powerful drug that people who are addicted to it can suffer very severe withdrawal symptoms if they do not keep taking it. This can actually be very dangerous for pregnant women addicted to heroin, since the symptoms of heroin withdrawal can be fatal not only to them but to their unborn babies as well.

Other drugs that can harm the unborn child include PCP, LSD, glues and solvents, amphetamines (speed), barbiturates, and tranquilizers. If you are pregnant and have used any of these drugs, stop taking them as soon as possible. Remember that there is more than one life at stake. If you use drugs, cigarettes, or alcohol because of pressure from friends, there are ways to say no. Take another look at Chapter 2 for information on effective communication and other peer-resistance skills.

New Adjustments

Once your baby is born, your life is immediately different. If you choose to breastfeed your baby, your new child will need to be nursed every 2 to 3 hours, 24 hours a day, for the first few months of her life. This means that every couple of hours, night or day, you must get up with your baby to see that she is well fed. If she is hungry, she will let you know by crying. In fact, crying is the one way your baby can communicate with you until she is about six weeks old, when you may find her smiling every once in a while.

Aside from being hungry, babies cry when they are tired, when their diapers are wet or dirty, and when they are in pain. Sometimes they may cry for no reason at all, which can be difficult and frustrating: It may seem that no matter what you do, your baby is still uncomfortable and miserable.

Some babies suffer from colic, which is acute abdominal pain caused by gas. Colicky babies (such as Tess's) often have crying jags every day at around the same time, usually late afternoon or early evening. The jags may last anywhere between one and four hours, and there is little anyone can do to ease the pain—or the noise.

Colic can be painful not only for babies but for their parents as well. It can be extremely difficult to hear your baby cry without being able to do anything about it. And the crying itself can be piercing and irritating. Most health care professionals recommend that the parents of a colicky child take turns being with the baby, while the other gets rest, preferably out of earshot of the baby (although this is not always possible). If you are on your own and your baby has colic, try to find a friend or relative who can help you during the crying jags and perhaps give you time away.

If you find yourself getting irritated with your baby, particularly during a crying jag, understand that what you are feeling is normal for anyone in those circumstances. But if you are tempted to strike your child or hurt her in any way, seek help from a doctor or health care professional immediately. Seeking help before any violence begins is absolutely crucial.

Parenting Day by Day

When you first get home from the hospital, your days and nights may be a little scattered. Sometimes they may even seem as though they're in reverse. Some babies sleep all day and are up for many hours at night. Sometimes there are things you can do to try to get your schedule back to normal—see your doctor for more information.

Around the age of three months to six months, your baby may have established a regular schedule. Even so, many babies are up early—around 5:30 A.M. or so. If you are nursing, your day begins as soon as your baby's does. If she isn't sleeping late, neither are you. When she wakes up, she will be hungry, and she'll need a diaper change. Your baby may then spend some time awake, or she may have an early morning nap. Again, when she wakes up, it will be time to feed and change her.

If you are in school or working, you may need to take time each morning to prepare several bottles for your baby to have during the day, when you are not around to feed her. If you have a relative, friend, or hired nurse to care for your baby at home, that person may be able to prepare formula bottles him- or herself. If you are breastfeeding your baby, you will need to find time during the day (one or two occasions) to either nurse your baby or to express milk from your breasts, using a special pump. Otherwise your breasts are likely to become engorged, or swollen, and may sometimes leak milk. Whether you are breastfeeding or not, you are likely to be tired when you come home after a full day at school or on the job. Keep in mind, however, that your baby still needs your care, even when you are tired. You will probably feed your baby two to four times between the time you get home and the time your baby goes to sleep at night.

Restless Nights

The schedule of eating and sleeping defines the daily routine for babies and their parents. Some babies eat more than others so that their mothers have to nurse every hour; other babies can go for as long as four or five hours between feedings. By the same token, there are some babies who sleep for most of the day and night, while others are constantly awake. Likewise, some babies develop a regular schedule, while others seem to follow no pattern.

The greatest struggle for many new parents is adjusting to nighttime awakenings. Sean, for example, was up every hour of the night, needing to be fed. When Valerie nursed him, he would sometimes go right back to sleep. Other times, however, he would remain awake, crying or cooing. Valerie and Trey, both exhausted, learned that one of them had to remain awake to be with Sean when he was. As it turned out, neither of them slept through the night for the first nine months of Sean's life.

Because he was a low birth-weight baby, Sean may have had special needs that made him especially difficult at night. But some healthy babies of normal weight are equally wakeful, cranky, or tired. Coping with nighttime situations are among the more relentless tasks that new parents have. This is part of what people mean when they say that parenting is a 24-hour-a-day job. As hard as it may seem, you need to be as loving, caring, and patient during the night (some of which never seem to end!) as you are during the day.

A New Type of Weekend

One of the hardest adjustments for some parents is getting used to the fact that weekends are no longer a time to rest and recuperate from the busy week that has just ended. Now, weekends are a time to be with your child—to take care of her, to watch her, to hold her. Once again, your day begins not when you choose, but when your child awakens, which can sometimes be as early as 5 A.M.

Tess found weekends hardest to deal with after Stephanie learned to crawl. Before that time, Stephanie was easier to control. Then one day, it seemed that Stephanie was every-where—in the kitchen, in the bathroom, getting in the cabinets underneath the sink—and Tess also had to be there to steer her back to safety. Again, this was a relentless, tiring task, one that got even worse after Stephanie learned to walk and the possibilities of danger increased. Sometimes friends would come over to keep Tess company, or Tess would take Stephanie out for a change of pace. But all the same, Saturdays and Sundays passed very slowly for Tess. Weekends, she knew, were no longer her own.

Changing Priorities

It may seem repetitive to say it again, but there really is no getting around the sacrifices parenthood entails. In addition to losing hours of sleep, leisure time, and restful weekends, you will probably have to say goodbye to certain activities, at least for the time being. Going to the movies, for example, which is something you may have taken for granted up until now, will be difficult if not impossible with a newborn baby. Parties with your friends will also be off limits, unless you can find a relative, friend, or babysitter to stay with your child while you are out.

Trey has dropped out of school because he needs to make more money. He's working full-time at a construction site, operating heavy machinery. He's been pulling double shifts lately to make more money. The work leaves him exhausted at the end of the day, both mentally and physically. He can barely stay awake long enough to talk to Valerie and does not have the energy to deal with Sean.

Valerie, on the other hand, is beginning to resent the way Trey just comes home and goes to sleep. All the work with Sean is left up to her. Trey's parents help, but they also work. At night, it's always up to Valerie. She can't remember the last time she went out with her friends—they've stopped calling to ask her over. And even if they did call, Valerie wouldn't be able to go. First of all, who would stay with Sean? Second, Valerie wants to spend the little time she has to herself resting. The sleepless nights and endless days have gotten to her. She's exhausted, and there doesn't seem to be an end in sight. At night, she wants to grab Trey and push him out of bed so that he can take care of Sean and let her sleep. But Trey just rolls over and goes back to sleep when Sean cries. "I'm the one who needs to work, Val," he says when she talks to him about it. "I need to be awake to do my job. Without the money, we'd be in huge trouble. You know that."

The Big Picture

The day-to-day demands of parenting will probably be the first issues you will confront with a new baby. Just as important, though, are the larger, life-long issues. For one thing, parenting is expensive. For another, as much as you may want to be with your child, there will be times when you can't possibly be there. Finding good day care providers is a concern that must be handled in order for you to go to school or to a job that will allow you to provide for your new family. For many parents, it is these big-picture concerns that require the most work and the greatest adjustments.

Economics

There are no two ways about it; having a baby costs lots of money. To begin with, there's the price of diapers. New babies tend to go through about 8 to 10 diapers a day. A store-brand package costs about $5 and contains about 40 diapers. This breaks down to about a dollar a day, which may not seem like much, but which finally comes out to $365 a year.

Then there is the cost of food. Until your baby is about four months old she will be consuming only breast milk or formula. Many mothers choose to nurse their children not only for the nutritional value of breast milk but also because of the vast expense of formula. A baby can go through a large can of formula in about a week. These cans cost anywhere from $8 to $10 each, so during those first 4 months, women who choose to bottle feed their babies must be able to budget up to $160 for that time.

After four months, the baby will begin eating food. Most babies eat about 6 to 8 jars a day of baby food, which cost about 50¢ each. That adds up to an additional $120 a month. Some parents make their own baby food, by mashing fresh fruits and vegetables themselves. This can save money, although it is time consuming.

Meanwhile, there are the costs of clothing and furniture. You can save on this by buying used goods, but count on spending at least $200 for a crib, a stroller, and some useful furniture or toys. Clothes are harder to price, and it could be that you can rely on hand-me-downs from a relative or friend. Even so, you will be amazed at how much a child needs in a year to stay appropriately dressed for all seasons —and how quickly she will outgrow the clothes you get for her.

Once your child is eating the same food you are and is out of diapers, these costs will diminish—but others may take their place. You may find yourself spending more on clothes and toys, for example. And depending on your health insurance, there may be medical bills to pay as well.

If you are working full-time, you may have health benefits from your job. If you don't, you may have to worry about either obtaining health insurance for your child, which can be very costly, or paying for medical expenses yourself, which is costlier still.

Welfare Revisited

As you learned in Chapter 1, there is a government program that has been specifically designed to help needy families meet the cost of living. That program, known as welfare, or Aid to Families with Dependent Children (AFDC), has made it easier for single parents in particular to raise their children. Not only does AFDC provide a monthly check for basic needs—though this check is very, very small—but it also offers health insurance, in the form of Medicaid.

Chapter 1 also discussed the new welfare regulations. As you learned, one of the requirements teen parents have to meet in order to receive payments is to live with at least one of their parents until they've reached the age of 21.

This arrangement has both advantages and disadvantages. Teenagers who come from supportive families may benefit from living at home not only financially but emotionally. Tess, for example, has actually grown closer to her mother since Stephanie was born. Her mother loves Stephanie as much as Tess does, and despite the difficulties, the three of them have become a happy family. But according to a 1996 report published by *Washington Monthly*, the majority of teen parents were raised in troubled homes. Two-thirds of these young parents, for example, were sexually abused—most by a member of their own family—before the age of 10. Of course it is unfair and unwise to force a teenager who has been abused by her family not only to live there but to raise her own child in that atmosphere.

Fortunately, there is an exemption to the new policy for teenagers in this situation. If you are seeking welfare support and are scared to live at home because you have been abused by your family, make sure you let your caseworker know of your situation. There is, for example, a program called Second Chance Homes, which provides shelter and supervision for teen mothers who have left abusive situations at home and are in need of welfare support.

Finally, the new welfare regulations are making a tremendous attempt to decrease the number of out-of-wedlock births. Single-parent families do not receive additional funds should they have another out-of-wedlock child. In addition, extra funds are now rewarded to five states each year who manage to show a decreased rate of out-of-wedlock births without increasing the abortion rate.

Day Care

If and when you do choose to return from full-time parenting to school or to a job, you will need to make some responsible decisions concerning the care of your child. Both Tess and Valerie have been able to work out situations where a family member watches their children while they go to school. There are several other options parents can explore. It's important to know, however, that finding proper day care is one of the hardest hurdles all parents face. This is often especially true for teen parents, who may not have the resources to pay for the best day care available in their area.

First, there are community centers, such as the YMCA, that often have day care programs at decent rates because they are subsidized by the government. Privately run centers can watch your child as well, but at a far higher cost.

Many states now have an accreditation system that rates all day care centers. If your state has such a system, you should be sure that the center you choose meets the minimal accreditation requirements. In any case, make a point of meeting the day care employees who will be spending time with your child. It's important that you know them and trust them—you are leaving the care of your child to them.

Some parents leave their children in an at-home day care facility. This is the home of a woman who cares for one to five children at a time, usually in her own home. Again, most states require at-home day care providers to be licensed. Be sure that the one you choose has a license and is, once again, a person you trust.

Many schools now provide on-campus day care for the children of its students and staff. For many teen parents, this is the easiest arrangement, because it allows them to be near their babies all day long and to visit them in between classes. If your school does have such an arrangement, you should let them know you're interested early on in your pregnancy so that there will be room for your child.

Teen Fathers

Most of what you read about teen parenthood, including much of this book, is addressed to the mother. This is because in the vast majority of cases, the mother is the primary care provider. That is not to say, however, that the plights, problems, and joys of both pregnancy and parenthood are completely off limits to teen fathers, even though historically they have been less involved with their children than the mothers have.

According to a study published in 1996 by the *Journal of Contemporary Human Services,* only 36 percent of teen mothers reported daily contact with the father of their child by the time the child was one month old. By the time the child was four-and-a-half years of age, that statistic had diminished to 20 percent.

In addition, there is an important distinction to be made between teen fathers—that is, boys who become fathers while they are teenagers themselves—and the fathers of babies born to teen mothers. The same *Journal of Contemporary Human Services* study found that almost 40 percent of the fathers in their sample were 20 years of age or older. A study done by the Alan Guttmacher Institute in 1995 similarly found that while 12 percent of unmarried new mothers in 1988 were between the age of 15 and 19, just 5 percent of the new fathers of the babies born to these mothers were that young.

Nevertheless, many teen fathers face the same emotional and financial burdens that teen mothers do. To begin with, studies show that teen fathers are just as unlikely to finish high school as teen mothers, and are likewise less financially successful than their peers who don't have children. Also, as you learned in Chapter 4, teen fathers can be held legally responsible for the financial well-being of their child, whether or not they are in contact with the child and mother.

Teen fathers who do live with their new family are subject to the same burdens and joys as teen mothers. They too have to cope with sleepless nights, sleepy mornings, lost weekends, crying jags, and other day-to-day issues of child care.

In addition, teen fathers have even less of a concrete way to prepare for the radical change of life they are about to experience. The mothers of their children go through a nine-month pregnancy in which their bodies change dramatically and they can feel their babies move inside them. Teenage boys can watch the pregnancy progress, but they don't experience it firsthand. When the baby comes, it may be even more of a shock to them than to teen mothers.

Moreover, there are far fewer resources for teen fathers to turn to than for teen mothers. Since far fewer teenage boys play an active role in the rearing of their children, they may have trouble finding kindred spirits and role models. Teen mothers have a much easier time finding support, both within the community and on a broader national level.

If you are a teen father in need of emotional support, however, there are ways to find it. Several states offer support groups, and there are handbooks for teen fathers as well. One of these handbooks, published by the Teen Father's Program of the Sacramento (California) YWCA, offers information that may help prepare teenagers who are about to become fathers and discusses options available for adolescents who have already had children. The handbook also gives some advice on ways that the teen father can offer support to the baby's mother, which both makes her life easier and helps the father to feel more needed and involved.

To find a support group for teenage fathers in your community, check the yellow pages of your phone book. If there isn't anything listed there, call your local family planning center, the YMCA, or a local youth center. Any of these may offer a support group themselves, or they might help you find one that suits your needs. See Chapter 7 for more resources for teen families.

Teen Marriage

Many people still have an old-fashioned image in mind when it comes to teen marriage: the father of a pregnant teenager pointing a gun at the girl's boyfriend, the one who has fathered her unborn child. "Marry her," the girl's father might be saying, "or you won't live to see the light of day." Scared out of his wits, the boy does what he's told—and everyone lives happily ever after.

For some teenage couples and their babies, this may in fact be the case. Studies show that the children who grow up in families with both a mother and a father are on the whole healthier and happier than those who grow up in single-parent situations. This is not surprising, given that single-parent families often have more stresses and fewer financial resources than do families with married parents. But it's important to remember that the children of unhappily married parents—particularly those who have married out of necessity, rather than for love—can be extremely unhappy themselves. For this reason and others, anyone planning to live together and particularly to embark on a marriage needs to know that this is as dramatic a change as having a child and often brings the same amount of responsibility.

As with being a parent, marriage or cohabitation (living together) requires a certain amount of selflessness—putting another person's needs before your own. This is especially true when there is a child involved. Compromise and selfishness are words that come up a lot when Valerie and Trey argue. Valerie is happy that Trey invited her to live with him, but there are times that she doesn't feel he's pulling his weight enough when it comes to Sean. Valerie has told Trey that she works just as hard at being a parent to their child as she would if Trey weren't in the picture. "When was the last time you changed his diaper? Or got up in the middle of the night with him?" she wants to know. "You know, you're just unbelievably selfish—you have no idea how to compromise." But Trey thinks Valerie's asking too much. "Look, I need to sleep at night. If I don't, how can I do my job the next day? And what would happen to all of us if I got fired? I'm the one working all the time. Maybe when you bring home some bucks I'll feel like helping you more with the kid. In the meantime, don't go around calling *me* selfish."

Chances are that Valerie probably does have it easier than single teenage mothers do. For one thing, she has a regular source of income, small as it may be, and a companion who does help raise Sean.

Nevertheless, Valerie and Trey are two teenagers involved in an adult relationship. Not only are they new parents, but they are now living together. The decisions they make have to be ones they can both live with and abide by. Living with a partner requires emotional maturity as well as the ability to make responsible decisions. (See Chapter 3 for more information on maturity and decision making.) Most teenagers are not yet ready for the level of self-sacrifice that a successful marriage requires. This may be one reason that according to the National Center for Health Statistics's 1995 fact sheet, marriages between teenagers are far more likely to end in divorce than those between adults.

Where You Can Go

As you know by now, being a teen parent involves sacrifice, both day to day and for years to come. Fortunately, there are resources available to help teenagers cope with the new lives they have chosen.

One such initiative is the Teen Parent Program (TPP) in Del Valle, Texas. This program works closely with the Del Valle school district to provide services and resources to teen parents who live in the community. The essential goals of the TPP initiative are the following:

- Improve teen parenting skills
- Improve child development
- Re-enroll teens in appropriate school programs, when necessary
- Help young parents attain self-sufficiency
- Assist families experiencing crises
- Reduce the number of repeat teen pregnancies

With these intentions in mind, TPP offers home visits to teens and their children on a weekly or biweekly basis. It also provides child-development assessments, which are check-ups on the developmental progress of the babies; family advocacy, which involves special representatives who are assigned to help families should such incidents as child or spouse abuse occur; and case management, which helps families locate needed services, such as medical care or legal representation. Finally, teenagers in Del Valle can receive free child care for their babies, transportation, competency-based secondary education, computer training, and cooperative summer school and work opportunities.

TPP was developed to serve a rural community where few teenagers drive and there is no public transportation available. The services provided to teenagers living there make life manageable for these new, young parents.

Unfortunately for teen parents, few communities have a program as well organized and effective as TPP. Still, there may be resources available that can help you get through the first few months of your child's life, as well as helping you explore options for the future. Check the listings in Chapter 7 of this book for possibilities.

6

The Search for Solutions

Tess's second baby was adopted by a family in another state. She thinks about her little boy all the time and feels sad when she realizes that she won't be there to watch him grow up—to see who he looks like, what makes him laugh, and what he likes to do for fun. At the same time, Tess is happy that her son is with a loving family—one that can do much more for him than she can.

What really disturbs Tess is seeing all the teenage girls in her neighborhood who are pregnant now. They act so overconfident, even cocky. Then there are the girls who are just beginning to go out with guys. Tess doesn't know them well enough to say anything to them, but if she did, she'd tell them to be careful. Pregnancy *is* a big deal. It changes your life, and makes it much harder.

Tonya and Jack have both graduated from high school, and they're headed in different directions. Tonya got a scholarship to go to a small college in another state, and

Jack has chosen to take some time off from school and work in his dad's store for a while. He hasn't decided yet if he wants to go to college. Both Tonya and Jack don't really know how they're going to deal with the separation. They've been talking about it for months, and they have finally decided that even though they are still together, they don't want to hold one another back.

At first Jack told Tonya that if she meets other guys at school he doesn't want her to go out with them, but Tonya said that wasn't fair. She said they both should date other people if they want to—they're too young to be tied down. Tonya knows that if Jack meets someone first it will hurt, but she also feels that she and Jack will end up together if it's right. She doesn't regret anything they've done. She's also happy that they acted responsibly. Tonya knows that if an accident had happened and she had gotten pregnant, she wouldn't have been able to take this scholarship. She and Jack would probably have gotten married, but Tonya thinks it would have been for the wrong reason. "We would have killed each other," she says. Much as he hates to admit it, Jack knows she's right. As much as they love one another, getting married and having a child right out of high school would probably have been really hard.

The good news about teen pregnancy is that it's on the decline. According to a 1997 study by the National Center for Health Statistics, teenage birthrates nationwide have diminished substantially from 1991 to 1996. The reason for this trend is unclear. Some credit a focus in education on the need to remain abstinent before marriage. "We believe abstinence has played the central role in what's happening." Amy Stephens, a spokeswoman for the pro-abstinence organization Focus in the Family, told the *New York Times* in a May 1, 1998 article. "Kids respond when they get a direct message [to remain abstinent] instead of the mixed message that if you're going to have sex, you should use a condom, but oh, also, we don't think you should have sex."

On the other hand, other groups stress that the proper use of contraceptives has been the key to the diminishing rate of teen pregnancy in the United States. "We're seeing the result of more widespread and more effective contraceptive use," Jacqueline E. Darroch, senior vice president for research at the Alan Guttmacher Institute, told the *New York Times* in the same article.

Even so, both national and community leaders believe that more work has to be done to bring down the rate of teen pregnancy even further. The keys to success, many strategists believe, is to offer a positive message to teenagers —one that stresses the advantages of postponing not only parenthood, but sexual involvement as well. As you read the ideas listed in this chapter, ask yourself whether they are realistic ones. Do you agree with the messages? Do you think most teenagers would agree with them?

The National Strategy to Prevent Teen Pregnancy

In 1995 President Clinton announced that the issue of teen pregnancy was a crucial one sorely in need of attention. He voiced concern not only for the social cost of teen pregnancy (see Chapter 1) but for its effects on both adolescent parents and their children. Clinton put his vision in specific terms: He strives to cut teen pregnancy rates by 33 percent by the year 2006.

With this mission in mind, the U.S. Department of Health and Human Services has issued a national strategy to achieve two specific goals. First, it stresses the need to encourage teenagers to avoid teen pregnancy. Second, it strives to use both local and national initiatives to remind teenagers that staying in school, delaying sexual inter-course, and preparing for work are, in the long run, the best things to do.

The Key Principles

The U.S. Department of Health's strategy stresses that the best way to prevent teen pregnancy is to carry out the following five principles through community-based prevention programs.

1) Parental and adult involvement: Increased communication between teenagers and trusted adults is key.
2) Abstinence: Any prevention program, the strategy stresses, must begin with a strong message to delay sexual intercourse.
3) Clear strategies for the future: Young people must be given realistic and attainable opportunities to attend college and pursue jobs.
4) Community involvement: The strategy stresses that all facets of a community—including parents, schools, businesses, media, health and human services providers, religious organizations, and of course, teenagers themselves—must work together to develop realistic and comprehensive prevention approaches.
5) Sustained commitment: Nothing works overnight. True success will come only if these principles are followed over a period of time.

Welfare Reform

As you learned in Chapter 1, the welfare law signed by President Clinton in 1996 includes specific policies for adolescent parents. In particular, it states that all teen mothers must live at home and stay in school in order to receive governmental assistance. The law also provides for Second Chance Homes, a program for teenagers at risk of being abused if they stay with their parents. The idea behind this program is to provide supervised group residences for teen mothers from abusive or unstable homes to live with their children. With money and guidance from the federal government, the homes provide socialization, nurturing, support, structure, and discipline for these young mothers and their children. All mothers who live in the Second Chance Homes network do qualify for welfare assistance.

In addition, the welfare law provides $50 million a year to fund state abstinence-education programs. This means that there will be more tools available to help teenagers make informed, responsible decisions to delay sexual intercourse until they are older.

Finally, the new policy intends to send a strong message to teenagers that parenthood does involve responsibility and obligations. With this goal in mind, the law includes measures to name the father in every case of teen pregnancy and to prosecute those fathers who are not paying proper child support.

In Chapter 1, you learned about the provisions of the new welfare law. Now that you've had a chance to read more about the issue of teen pregnancy, have you changed your opinion about that law?

Government Initiatives

For a project at school, Tess is trying to learn all she can about what the U.S. government is doing to try to limit the number of teen pregnancies in the United States. Tess understands that the government has a long way to go in achieving their goal of minimizing teen pregnancy, but so far she likes what she sees.

Tess has found that there are a number of initiatives that are funded by the federal government, and the good news is that teenagers don't have to go to Washington, D.C. in order to benefit from the programs because there are branches of these programs in communities all over the United States. Another thing Tess likes about the initiatives is that they focus not only on preventing pregnancy but on helping teenagers who are already pregnant or have children by providing them information and services.

For example, the Adolescent Family Life Program is an organization that supports projects to advocate abstinence.

The AFL puts this first on its agenda because abstinence is the only sure way to prevent not only pregnancy but the spread of all sexually transmitted diseases. But as Tess knows, many teenagers do have sexual intercourse. What about services for them? Tess was happy to find that the AFL also offers some health, education, and social services to teen mothers who are either pregnant or already parents, as well as to their infants, male partners, and families. (It's important to note, however, that current restrictions do not allow any federally funded family planning services to discuss the option of abortion.) Finally, the AFL sponsors in 14 states projects that are specifically designed to reduce repeat teen pregnancy through education.

Great, Tess thinks to herself when she reads about this last part of the AFL goal, so where were you when I needed you? She knows that a lot of teens would love to use these initiatives but don't even know they exist. These programs, she thinks to herself, should be in schools so that teenagers don't have to go out and find them for themselves.

Fortunately, the government is taking steps to implement programs in schools as well as in community centers. One initiative, called Healthy Schools, Healthy Communities, has established health centers in schools in 27 communities in 20 states and the District of Columbia. These centers, Tess discovered, provide a wide range of educational and health-related services for teenagers who are considered at a high risk of becoming pregnant. There are also community school programs, again funded by the federal government, that support activities during nonschool hours for young people in communities that have a high number of pregnant teenagers. Finally, there are funded school programs designed specifically to reduce early sexual activity and abuse of tobacco, alcohol, and illicit drugs.

State and Community Prevention Strategies
Tess has also found other government initiatives, such as those that help teenagers deal with substance abuse, and

some hot lines for pregnant teens that she knows will be helpful for teenagers. But she also feels that any successful effort to reduce teen pregnancy really needs to begin on the community, or grassroots, level. That way, community residents are involved from the beginning. In addition, there are so many different communities in the United States, it seems to Tess, that the best way to find a program that suits the economic and social needs of a given community is for residents of that community to come up with a program themselves.

It's true that the most important strategies for pregnancy prevention are not the ones that originate in Washington, D.C., but the ones that happen at the grassroots level. The idea behind grassroots projects is to help provide opportunities for the community's teenagers to be educated about pregnancy and also to provide options for them and their future. In other words, successful community programs to reduce teenage pregnancy aim to provide teenagers with hope and opportunity. In Chapter 1 you learned that one reason teenagers get pregnant may be out of a sense of hopelessness. Perhaps if teenagers are provided with some guidance and support, fewer teenagers will resort to pregnancy as a "quick fix" to relieve the pain and hopelessness about their future that they may be feeling.

With these goals in mind, several communities have started innovative programs to help their teenage residents. For example, the Washington State Department of Health has spearheaded the Teen Pregnancy Prevention Media Campaign. This program, according to the website of Washington's Ferndale High School (http://168.212.80.25/TeenAware/tppmco.html), had five specific goals:

- "To develop a sense of responsibility, commitment, and ownership of the issue in individual communities across the state.
- To encourage teens to delay sexual activity or to use contraceptives if they are already sexually active.

- To provide information to the public regarding the facts and issues about teen pregnancy.
- To encourage parents and other influential adults to exercise responsibility for their children's behavior.
- To promote collaboration and communication among schools, community organizations, and private partnerships, including cross training, joint planning, and resource pooling."

In order to meet these ambitions, the campaign will use several different media outlets: radio commercials developed by teens and conveying specific messages, such as the consequences of early sexual activity, to be played on popular teen stations; tabloid inserts and advertisements on teen issues, to be published in a popular teen newspaper; and televised town hall meetings on teen issues, including parent-teen communication and responsible sexual behavior.

There are some other innovative community programs as well. For example, in New York City Dr. Michael Carrera has initiated a pregnancy prevention program that provides tutoring, college tuition, and classes in sex and health education to participating teenagers. His program, which has been adopted in several other states, is based on the positive philosophy that the way to help teenagers avoid pregnancy is to offer them opportunities that give them hope and possibilities for a better future.

Another promising campaign to reduce pregnancy is under way in Arkansas, where the media have spearheaded a statewide effort to alert residents about the problem of teen pregnancy and to encourage them to take preventative action. With this goal in mind, the state has implemented prevention and parenting programs in five communities. One program focuses on ways parents can talk to their children about sex. Another offers pregnancy prevention workshops to male teenagers and young adults. A third strives to prevent second pregnancies through employment opportunities and self-esteem classes.

Prevention Through Limitations

Many lawmakers believe that the best way to prevent teen pregnancy is to make it harder for teen parents to receive the benefits they have always counted on to help them raise their children, such as welfare, for example. In addition, these lawmakers believe that punishing teens and young adults for their actions will serve as a useful prevention technique. Several states have taken action to test this theory. For example,

- In Iowa, all teen parents are required by law to live at home or under adult supervision. In addition, they must attend parenting classes, complete high school, and participate in PROMISE JOBS, Iowa's job training program.
- In Maryland, legislation is pending that would require all unmarried teen parents to live under adult supervision.
- California has established the Underage Sex Offense Unit, which investigates and prosecutes adult males who impregnate teenagers and younger girls.
- In Florida, legislation is pending that would charge a man over 18 who has impregnated a girl under the age of 15 with second-degree statutory rape. The offender would be responsible for child support and medical costs related to pregnancy.

Principles Behind Prevention

What do you think is the best strategy to reduce teen pregnancy in your community? Do you believe in discouraging teenagers by making it more difficult for them to receive financial support should they ever become parents? Or are you in favor of providing teenagers with hope and opportunities for the future so that they won't turn to irresponsible sexual behavior—and often pregnancy—as an immediate source of happiness?

If the second of these choices seems to be the more appealing, keep in mind that it is very difficult to change the realities of life in the inner cities and in rural towns with few activities—to offer teenagers and others a way out of what they may find to be a depressing and unbearable way of life.

At the same time, don't lose sight of the fact that it can be done. Options do exist for impoverished teenagers, mainly in the form of education and community activities. You might consider becoming involved in community-wide efforts to reduce teen pregnancy, as well as in efforts to combat drug and alcohol abuse among teenagers. Not only will you feel good about yourself for participating in these efforts, but you may find that you have met people and done things that can provide you with more ideas and options for your own future.

It's important to remember that the real prevention strategy for teen pregnancy is not found in either communities or federal programs. Instead, it is ultimately within the control of teenagers themselves to decide what they want to do and how they want to live their lives. It's easy to cite statistics on what the best decisions are: that having a baby while you're still a teenager will make it harder for you to finish your education, and by extension will limit your opportunities as an adult. But finally, no one can dictate your actions but you yourself. You have the power to take a hard look at the information you have and then to make a responsible decision based on that knowledge.

Weighing Your Options

When you are making choices regarding your life, keep in mind some of the information and strategies you've learned from this book. For example, you've probably always known that practicing sexual abstinence is the one and only sure way to prevent pregnancy from occurring. But what you may not have been aware of is that there are skills involved that can help you make the decision to practice abstinence, and to follow through on that decision in the face of internal and external pressures.

Making the decision to practice abstinence requires high self-esteem and a solid sense of confidence. It also calls for good communication skills, as well as the ability to resolve conflict and to resist peer pressure. But of all the skills described here, the most valuable one may be the ability to make a responsible decision. Making the decisions that are right for you is one way to work for the life you want, now and as an adult.

Remember that it's never too late to become responsible and to reflect that responsibility in the decisions you make. If, for example, you choose to become sexually active while still a teenager, there are steps you can take to lessen (but not eliminate) your chances of becoming pregnant. Birth control can be effective when used correctly every time.

If you have already become pregnant, responsible decision making will help you make the difficult choice of what path to take. Your options are abortion, adoption, or keeping the child and raising him or her yourself. None of these choices are easy ones; all require serious thought and consideration of the advantages and disadvantages so that, whatever their consequences, you will know you made the decision that was right for you.

Should you become a teen parent, keep in mind that your responsibility is just beginning. The ability to make a sound decision is more crucial now than ever before, because rather than just taking care of yourself, you have a baby who depends on you for survival and support. At the same time, you still do need to keep making sound decisions for yourself. If you are already the parent of one child, for example, you have choices to make and steps to take in order to prevent another pregnancy from occurring.

Making decisions unselfishly, which is required of parents of every age, is harder to do as a teenager than as an adult, but it can be done. There are places you can go to—and people you can talk to—for help with that difficult task. For more on places to go for help and support, see Chapter 7.

It may seem hard to believe, but in reality, you're at a very exciting time of life. On the brink of adulthood, you are just now learning what kind of gifts you have, and what kinds of things bring out the best in you. The greatest thing you can do for yourself is to remember that you have a tremendous amount of control over your own destiny. You have plenty of time to make some decisions about whether you want a family, a career, or both. Trust in yourself, and in your potential to be an adult with something to contribute to the world. And if you plan to be a parent, remember that it may well be your most difficult endeavor. If you have the emotional maturity and the ability to focus your energy and talent toward raising a child, it may well be your proudest accomplishment. It's your future; define it yourself.

7

Where to
Find Help

Family Planning

The following organizations can offer advice, information, and/or referrals to both female and male teens for issues concerning teen pregnancy.

Alan Guttmacher Institute
120 Wall Street
New York, NY 10005
(212) 248-1111

Association for Maternal and Child Health Programs
275 East Main Street
Frankfort, KY 40621
(502) 564-4830

Maternal and Child Health Bureau
5600 Fishers Lane

Parklawn Building, Room 18A-59
Rockville, MD 20857
(301) 443-8041

Nation Network for Youth Information
1319 F Street NW, Suite 401
Washington, DC 20004
(202) 783-7949

National Organization of Adolescent Pregnancy, Parenting
  and Prevention
4421A East-West Highway
Bethesda, MD 20814
(301) 913-0378

Office of Adolescent Pregnancy Programs
PHS, Department of Health and Human Services
4350 East-West Highway, Suite 200 West Towers
Bethesda, MD 20814
(301) 594-4004

Parent Aid and Family Support Center
427 West 12th Street
Juneau, AK 99801
(907) 586-3785

Planned Parenthood Federation of America
810 Seventh Avenue
New York, NY 10019
(212) 541-7800

Planned Parenthood Ottawa
1390 Prince of Wales Drive, Suite 409
Ottawa, Ontario
Canada K2C 3N6
(613) 226-3234

SAFE Inc. (Sexual Abstinence & Family Education)
3040 Continental Drive, Suite 300
Butte, MT 59701
(406) 494-2174

Sexuality Information and Education Council of the
  United States (SIECUS)
130 West 42 Street, Suite 350
New York, NY 10036
(212) 819-9770

The two websites that follow also discuss teen pregnancy.

Coalition for Positive Sexuality
http://www.positive.org

Teen Help
http://www.vpp.com/teenhelp

Abortion

The following organizations can offer information about abortion to teenagers exploring options, as well as to people interested in the pro-choice–pro-life debate.

Pro-Choice

Canadian Abortion Rights Action League (CARAL)
One Nicholas Street, Suite 726
Ottawa, Ontario
Canada KIN 7B7
(613) 789-9956

National Abortion Rights Action League (NARAL)
1156 15th Street NW, Seventh Floor
Washington, DC 20005
(202) 973-3000

National Abortion Federation
1436 W Street NW, Suite 103
Washington, DC 20009
(202) 667-5882

Pro-Life

Americans United for Life
343 South Dearborn, Suite 1804
Chicago, IL 60604
(312) 786-2131

National Right to Life Committee
419 Seventh Street NW, Suite 500
Washington, DC 20004

Right to Life of Kitchener-Waterloo
380 King Street North
Waterloo, Ontario
Canada N2J273
(519) 746-5433

Consult these websites too.

Reproductive Health and Rights Center
http://www.choice.org

Ultimate Pro-Life Resource List
http://www.prolife.org

Adoption

The following organizations offer information to pregnant teens about the option of adoption.

Adoption Information Services
P.O. Box 82706

Kenmore, WA 98208
(206) 325-9500

National Council for Adoption
Director
1930 17th Street NW
Washington, DC 20009
(202) 328-1200

Here are a couple of websites.

AdoptioNetwork
http://www.adoption.org

Adoption Resource Network
http://www.arni.org

Rape, Sexual Assault, and Abuse

The following organizations offer information about rape, sexual assault, and abuse, and help for those in need.

National Coalition Against Sexual Assault
912 North Second Street
Harrisburg, PA 17102
(202) 483-7165

Rape Crisis Center
5835 Callaghan Road, Suite 260
San Antonio, TX 78228
(210) 349-7273 (hot line)
(210) 521-7273 (business)

Rape and Domestic Violence Information Center
P.O. Box 4228

Morgantown, WV 26505
(304) 292-5100
(800) 554-9743

National Child Abuse Hot Line
(800) 422-4453

National Rape Hot Line
(800) 656-HOPE

Ottawa Rape Crisis Centre
P.O. Box 20206
Ottawa, Ontario
Canada KIN 9P4
(613) 562-2333

Following are some websites to visit.

Rape and Sexual Harassment Resources
http://www.igc.apc.org/women/activists/harass.html

Rape: Get Help
http://www.ocs.mq.edu.au/~korman/feminism/Rape/
get_help.html

Sexually Transmitted Diseases

The following organizations offer information and advice about sexually transmitted diseases.

AIDS Hot Line
(800) 342-2437
(800) 344-7432 (Spanish)

American Social Health Association
P.O. Box 13827
Research Triangle Park, NC 27709
(919) 361-8400

Health and Welfare Canada/Secretariat National Sur le SIDA
  (AIDS)
Edifice Jeanne Mance, Room 1742
Parc Tunney
Ottawa, Ontario
Canada K1A069
(613) 952-5258

National STD Hot Line
(800) 227-8922

Public Health Service
Centers for Disease Control and Prevention
U.S. Public Health Service
1600 Clifton Road, NE
Atlanta, GA 30333
(404) 329-3534

Sexuality Information and Education Council of the United
  States (SIECUS)
80 Fifth Avenue, Suite 801
New York, NY 10011
(212) 929-2300

You can also consult the following websites.

Information for People with Sexually Transmitted Diseases
http://www.eastend.com.au

What Women Should Know About Sexually Transmitted
  Diseases
http://www.aomc.org

Welfare

The following organizations provide information about welfare.

Center on Social Welfare Policy and Law
275 Seventh Avenue, Suite 1203
New York, NY 10001
(212) 633-6967

National Health and Welfare Union
233 Gilmour Street, Suite 1202
Ottawa, Ontario
Canada K2P OP2
(613) 237-2732

Here are two websites about welfare.

Welfare Reform (Department of Health and Human Services)
http://www.acf.dhhs.gov

Child Welfare Resource List
http://www.gahsc.org

For Further Reading

The following titles provide additional information about the issues surrounding teenage pregnancy.

Angel, Ronald J., and Jacqueline L. Angel. *Painful Inheritance: Health and the New Generation of Fatherless Families.* Madison, Wis.: University of Wisconsin Press, 1993.

Bell, Ruth. *Changing Bodies, Changing Lives: A Book for Teens on Sex and Relationships.* Rev. ed. New York: Vintage Books, 1988

Bode, Janet. *Kids Still Having Kids: People Talk About Teen Pregnancy.* New York: Franklin Watts, 1992.

Brown, Fern G. *Teen Guide to Childbirth.* New York: Franklin Watts, 1988.

Calderone, Mary S., and Eric W. Johnson. *The Family Book About Sexuality.* Rev. ed. New York: Harper and Row, 1989.

DuPrau, Jeanne. *Adoption: The Facts, Feelings, and Issues of a Double Heritage.* Englewood Cliffs, N.J.: Julian Messner, 1990.

Eisenberg, Arlene, Heidi Murkoff, and Sandee Hathaway. *What to Expect When You're Expecting.* New York: Workman Publishing, 1990.

Emmens, Carol A. *The Abortion Controversy.* Englewood Cliffs, N.J.: Julian Messner, 1987.

Guernsey, JoAnn Bren. *Teen Pregnancy.* New York: Clarion Books, 1989.

Jacobson, Cathy. *Think About: Teen Pregnancy.* New York: Walker, 1988.

Lindsay, Jeanne Warren. *Open Adoption: A Caring Option.* Buena Park, Calif.: Morning Glory Press, 1987.

Luker, Kristin. *Dubious Conceptions: The Politics of Teenage Pregnancy.* Cambridge, Mass.: Harvard University Press, 1996.

Kaufman, Gershen, and Lev Raphael. *Stick Up for Yourself! Every Kid's Guide to Personal Power and Positive Self-Esteem.* Minneapolis: Free Spirit Publishing, 1990.

Mufson, Susan, and Rachel Kranz. *Straight Talk About Date Rape.* New York: Facts On File, 1993.

Polakow, Valerie. *Lives on the Edge: Single Mothers and Their Children in the Other America.* Chicago: University of Chicago Press, 1993.

Scott, Sharon. *How to Say No and Keep Your Friends: Peer Pressure Reversal for Teens and Preteens.* Amherst, Mass.: Human Resource Development Press, 1988.

Silverstein, Herma. *Teenage and Pregnant: What You Can Do.* Englewood Cliffs, N.J.: Julian Messner, 1988.

Terkel, Susan Neiburg. *Finding Your Way: A Book About Sexual Ethics.* New York: Franklin Watts, 1993.

INDEX

Page numbers in *italics* indicate illustrations.